RULERS OF INDIA

RULERS OF INDIA

SIR THOMAS MUNRO

AND THE BRITISH SETTLEMENT OF THE MADRAS PRESIDENCY

BY

JOHN BRADSHAW, M.A., LL.D.

Inspector of Schools, Madras

GYAN

Published by

GYAN

Gyan Publishing House
5, Ansari Road
Daryaganj, New Delhi-110002
Phone: 011-47034999, 9811692060
E-mail: books@gyanbooks.com

Distribution Network
gyanbooks.com
India, USA, Canada, UK, Australia, France

ISBN : 978-81-212-4101-4 (PB)
First Published, 1894

2nd Impression 2020

Printed at: Gyan Press, Delhi.

Rulers of India
Author: Sir Thomas Munro

RULERS OF INDIA

Sir Thomas Munro

AND THE BRITISH SETTLEMENT OF THE MADRAS PRESIDENCY

BY

JOHN BRADSHAW, M.A., LL.D.

Inspector of Schools, Madras

Oxford

AT THE CLARENDON PRESS: 1894

SINCE this work was printed, news of the death of the Author has reached England. John Bradshaw devoted twenty-five years to education in India, twenty-three of them as a Professor or Inspector of Schools in the Madras Presidency. A scholarly man of letters and a patient searcher into the local sources of Indian history, he leaves a memory which will be cherished by many friends, but his sudden death deprives the world of the harvest of his long labours. With characteristic zeal he had given up the brief holiday at the beginning of the Indian year to verifying certain historical data in South Arcot, although it was known that cholera had broken out in that District. He returned to Madras with the disease upon him, and there died on January 5, 1894. So passes away another original worker in India, before accomplishing what seemed to be his life's-task.

W. W. H.

Feb. 11, 1894.

INTRODUCTION

No name, in any part of India, perhaps, is so familiar or held in such veneration as that of Munro is in the Madras Presidency, though two generations have passed away since his death. In the town of Madras the celebrated equestrian statue by Chantrey serves as a landmark, ever keeping the name of 'Munro' in the mouths of all; but in the Districts where the best years of his life were spent no monument is needed to perpetuate his name or memory.

Great changes have taken place in Southern India during the two-thirds of a century since Munro's death. The country has been opened up by railways and telegraph wires, and the people have been modernized by schools and colleges. Almost every town which Munro visited as Collector, Colonel, and Governor has now a railway station or is within a few hours' drive of one, and each has its English school, its dispensary or hospital, its post and telegraph office, its magistrate's court and its police station.

But great as have been the changes since Munro's time, they are not so great as those which the

Presidency witnessed in the half century between Thomas Munro's arrival at Madras as a military cadet in 1780, and his death as Governor in 1827. In the former year Haidar was devastating the Karnátik up to the walls of Fort St. George, and 'black columns of smoke were everywhere in view from St. Thomas' Mount.' During the following forty years the history of Madras was one of wars, of cession of territory to the British, and of the settlement of the new Districts. How large a share Munro took as a soldier and as a civil administrator in the British settlement of Southern India, these pages will show.

They will also exhibit a character worthy of imitation by every Indian official and by every well-wisher of the Indian races. His own letters paint the man—brave, wise, and kindly. No truer estimate of his qualities could be given than that by the Hon. Mountstuart Elphinstone—'strong practical good sense, simplicity and frankness, perfect good nature and good humour, real benevolence unmixed with the slightest cant of misanthropy, activity and truthfulness of mind, easily pleased with anything, and delighted with those things that in general have no effect but on a youthful imagination [1].'

'It is not enough,' the same writer observes, 'to give new laws or even good courts. You must take the people along with you, and give them a *share in your feelings*, which can only be done by *sharing*

[1] Colebrooke's *Life of Mountstuart Elphinstone*, ii. 35.

theirs.' This Munro did fully, and he had his reward, for to this day the natives of his old Districts rise up and call him blessed. In my official capacity I have visited almost every spot in the Madras Presidency in which Sir Thomas Munro lived or encamped, and can speak from personal knowledge of the impression that great administrator has left on the face of the country, the system on which it is governed, and on the hearts of the people. From Salem the Rev. W. Robinson, writing to me, says: 'Munro's name is held in the greatest reverence in this District, and the highest compliment they can pay a civilian is to compare him to Munro. I have talked to old natives who cherish his memory as that of their greatest benefactor.' In the Ceded Districts boys are still named after him, 'Munrolappa.' In the Cuddapah District wandering mendicants sing ballads to his praise. At Gooty a Bráhman schoolmaster recently informed me that 'Sir Thomas Munro is styled Mandava Rishi,—Mandava Rishi being no other than Munro deified.' In the recent season of scarcity, 1891–92, at a meeting held at Gooty, with the object of petitioning Government for a reduction of the land assessment, near the end of the proceedings an old *ráyat* stood up and merely said in Telugu, 'Oh for Munro Sáhib back again!'

As Munro's own letters afford the truest and the most vivid record of his life's work. they have been largely used in the following pages. They give this volume an autobiographical character which forms its individual feature in the Rulers of India Series. In his diary, Feb. 15, 1830, Elphinstone writes:—

'I have begun Sir T. Munro's *Life*, and am quite enchanted with it. It cannot fail to delight even those who had previously no interest in the subject. It is almost all made up of his own letters, which have fortunately been preserved, and which show that his judgment and sagacity at nineteen were as superior to those of ordinary people as they were to those of his contemporaries when his reputation was more extensive. They also most fortunately disclose the many accomplishments which were concealed by his modesty and that delicacy of taste and tenderness of feeling which lay hid under his plain and somewhat stern demeanour.'

This Memoir is mainly based on the *Life of Sir Thomas Munro*, by the Rev. G. R. Gleig, M.A., late Chaplain-General of the Forces (Colburn and Bentley), 3 vols. 1831, and the Letters have been reprinted from the revised edition, published in one volume by John Murray, 1849. The reader is also referred to Sir A. J. Arbuthnot's *Sir Thomas Munro, with Selections from his Minutes, &c.*, (Kegan Paul and Co., 1881); to Sir W. W. Hunter's *Brief History of the Indian Peoples*, and to the volumes on *Elphinstone* and the *Marquess of Hastings* in this Series.

Writing in India I have not had the advantage of seeing the final proofs of this work, but I desire to thank the Editor of the Series for his kindness and for the additional trouble he has had in seeing it through the press.

J. B.

MADRAS, *Oct.* 18, 1893.

CONTENTS

NOTE ON THE VOWEL SOUNDS

The orthography of proper names follows generally the system adopted by the Indian Government for the *Imperial Gazetteer of India*. That system, while adhering to the popular spelling of very well-known places, such as Punjab, Poona, Deccan, &c., employs in all other cases the vowels with the following uniform sounds:—

a, as in wom*a*n : *á*, as in f*a*ther : *i*, as in k*i*n : *í*, as in intr*i*gue : *o*, as in cold : *u*, as in b*u*ll : *ú*, as in r*u*ral.

SIR THOMAS MUNRO

CHAPTER I

BOYHOOD

THOMAS MUNRO was born in Glasgow on May 27, 1761. His father, Alexander Munro, was a merchant trading chiefly with Virginia, and his mother was sister of Dr. Stark, a well-known anatomist of that day. Thomas was the second child of a family of five sons and two daughters. In his infancy a severe attack of measles caused partial deafness; to this deafness he refers in his first letter from India, and to the increase of it, as he advanced in life, he makes frequent allusion in the correspondence of his later years.

Munro passed from the Grammar School to the Glasgow University, which he entered when he was about thirteen, remaining in it for nearly three years. At college he was distinguished in mathematics and chemistry, and was besides a great reader of history and literature apart from his collegiate course. Evidence of his literary taste and wide reading is disclosed in many of his private letters, a taste which he kept up throughout his life in India, showing himself no mean critic of the current literature of the day. Among the books or authors named by his biographer as his favourites were Anson's *Voyages*, Plutarch's *Lives*, Spenser, Shakespeare, Smith's *Wealth of Nations*, Hume's *History*, and the *Life of Frederick the Great*. Accounts of wars and of the tactics of generals afforded him peculiar interest. In order to read *Don Quixote* in the original when a boy he taught himself Spanish with the help of a dictionary and a grammar. This knowledge soon proved useful, for being the only person known to have a knowledge of the language, he was called on to translate some papers found in a Spanish vessel captured by a privateer belonging to a mercantile house in Glasgow. The reward which he received for this he gave to his mother as his first earnings.

Munro was well fitted by nature for the career he was destined to fill as a soldier and administrator in India. Tall and robust, he excelled in all athletic sports, and was possessed of a high courage, extraordinary agility, great presence of mind and powers of self-denial. Munro spent most of his vacations at a country house called Northwoodside, then two or three miles out of Glasgow. This spot was beautifully situated on the banks of the Kelvin, and the days he spent here fishing in the stream, or swimming in Jackson's dam, are often referred to in his correspondence from India.

In 1777 Munro's father obtained for him a clerkship in the counting-house of Messrs. Somerville & Gordon; West-Indian merchants in Glasgow. Shortly afterwards, the magistrates, who were not unacquainted with young Munro's military propensities, made him a tender of a lieutenancy in the corps which they were raising. But his father being opposed to his acceptance of it he reluctantly declined the offer, his disappointment being increased by the departure for military service of several of his old companions, one being the future Sir John Moore who died at Corunna.

In the following year, however, the house of which his father was a partner became embarrassed. The passing of the Act of Confiscation by the Congress of the United States led to its stopping payment, and the Munro family were reduced to comparative poverty. The father was now glad to accept for his son a midshipman's berth in the mercantile marine of the East India Company; but just before he sailed he was able to get it changed for a cadetship. Not being able to afford to pay for his passage, young Munro obtained permission from the captain of the *Walpole* to work his way out to Madras as an ordinary seaman [1], and here he arrived on January 15, 1780.

The following extract from a letter to his mother gives a humorous account of his first experiences after landing at Madras:—

[1] This incident Mr. Gleig was not aware of when he wrote his *Life of Sir Thomas Munro* in 1829, but mentions it in the edition of 1849.

'Dear Madam,

'When the ship anchored in the Roads, a number of the natives came on board. They were dressed in long white gowns. One of them, a grave, decent-looking man, came up to me; he held a bundle of papers in his hand, which he begged I would read; they were certificates from different people of his fidelity and industry. He said that strangers on their arrival in India were often at a loss for many necessary articles, but that I need give myself no trouble, for if I would only give him money, he would purchase for me whatever I wanted; he would attend me as a servant, and would be content with such wages as I should think upon trial he deserved. I congratulated myself on having met with so respectable a person in the character of a servant. He said he would go on shore and get me another, for that no gentleman could do without two, and that he would at the same time carry my dirty linen to be washed. I had only a few changes clean; I gave him the rest.

'Two days after, when I went on shore, I found my old man standing on the beach with half a dozen of porters to carry my baggage to Captain Henderson's house. I went early to sleep, quite happy at being rid of my old shipmates the soldiers.

'My servant entered the room while I was dressing next morning. He surveyed me, and then my bed, with amazement. The sea-chest, which occupied one half of the chamber, was open; he looked into it and shook his head. I asked the cause of his wonder.

"Oh, Sir, this will never do; nobody in this country wears buff waistcoats and breeches, or thread stockings, nor sleeps upon mattresses; sheets and blankets are useless in this warm climate; you must get a table and chairs, and a new bed."

'I was vexed to learn that all the clothes, of which I had taken so much care in the passage from Europe, were now to be of no service.

'He inspected the contents of the chest. The whole was condemned, together with the bed-clothes, as unserviceable, except three or four changes of linen which were to serve me till a tailor should fit me out in a proper manner.

'"It is customary with gentlemen," said the old man, "to make a present of all their European articles to their servants, but I will endeavour to dispose of yours to advantage; four guineas will buy a table and chairs, and cloth for the tailor, and as Captain Henderson is gone to Bengal, you must get a couch of your own; it will not cost above two guineas." He went out with the six guineas, leaving me with an empty chest, and my head full of new cuts of sleeves and skirts, which the tailor was to make in a few days. But all my schemes were disconcerted by some unfortunate accident befalling my good friend with the credentials, for he never returned.

'This unexpected blow prevented me from stirring out above twice or thrice in a week for several months after. On these days I sallied forth in a clean suit, and visited all my friends. After Dr. Koenig came to live with Mr. Ross, I spent the greatest part of my time at his house, amusing myself with shells and flowers; but before that I employed it differently.

'I rose early in the morning to review my clothes; after having determined whether shirt No. 3 or 4 was best, I worked at my needle till breakfast. When it was over I examined the cook's accounts, and gave orders about dinner; I generally read the rest of the day till the evening, when I mounted to the top of the house to observe the stars I had been reading of during the day in Ferguson's *Astronomy*.

'While I remained in Madras, my pay as a cadet was eight pagodas [1] a month; of this I gave two to a servant called a dubash, one to a cook, and one to the washerman; the remaining four were to answer every expense in a place where everything is sold at the highest price.

'With all my economy, it was near six months before I could save money enough to buy me a few suits of linen. I did not choose then to ask any of Mr. R.; and Mr. H. did not seem disposed to give me any assistance till I should leave Madras. But Mr. R., wishing to get me appointed to join the detachment under Colonel Baillie, I continued in Madras, making application for this purpose, till Haidar entered the Karnátik, when I joined the army in the field.'

[1] A pagoda was worth about 7s. 6d.

CHAPTER II

War with Haidar Alí

Sir Thomas Munro's life and work in India may be divided into four periods. The first, from 1780 to 1792, was purely military, and during most of these twelve years he was on active service in the wars with Haidar Alí and Tipú Sultán. In the second, 1792–1807, he was employed in the civil administration of the country: from 1792 to 1799 in the Bárámahal, which had been ceded by Tipú; in 1799–1800 in Kánara, and from 1800 to 1807 in the Districts still known as the Ceded Districts, acquired by treaty with the Nizám in 1800. The third period, 1814–1818, after an interval of six years in Europe, was spent partly in civil and partly in military duty. He was sent out by the Court of Directors in 1814 as 'Principal Commissioner for the revision of the internal administration of the Madras territories'—judicial and financial; and during 1817–1818 he was in command of a division of the army in the last Maráthá War. The fourth period, after a short visit to England in 1819, was that of his governorship of Madras from June 8, 1820, until his death on July 6, 1827.

The year in which Munro arrived at Madras was the commencement of a critical period in the history of British India. The conduct of the Madras Government—Sir Thomas Rumbold, the Governor, and Sir Hector Munro, the Commander-in-Chief, being at variance with the other members of Council—gave an opening which neither the French nor the other enemies of English supremacy were slow to make use of. Haidar Alí of Mysore, and the Nizám of the Deccan, the two strongest Musalmán powers in India, endeavoured to draw the Maráthás into an alliance against England, but the diplomacy of Hastings won over the Nizám and the Maráthá Rájá of Nágpur.

Haidar, at the head of a numerous and well-appointed army, joined by a corps of Europeans under Lally, marched from Seringapatam, and by August had laid siege to Arcot, a town about sixty-five miles west of Madras. 'The Government,' writes Munro in a letter to his father in October, 1780, 'being at length convinced by the burning of the villages around, and the country people daily flocking in multitudes to Madras, that Haidar had passed the mountains, prepared to oppose him. General Munro was ordered to take the command of the army, and at the same time instructions were sent to the north to Colonel Baillie to march with his detachment and join the main body.' Sir Hector Munro reached Conjeveram, and Colonel Baillie had advanced to within fourteen miles of the latter, when Haidar threw his army between the two and completely routed Baillie's detachment at Perambákam on September 10, 1780.

During the remainder of the war with Haidar and the French, Munro was actively employed, and in the Appendix will be found a 'Memorandum of his Services,' in which he gives a summary of his career in the army and while in civil employ. Throughout the war with Haidar, and subsequently during the wars with Tipú and with the Maráthás, Munro wrote long letters or journals to his father and to some of his friends, describing very fully the several campaigns and giving accounts of the battles and various military operations in which he was engaged. These letters not only possess the advantage of being written by an eye-witness, and at the time or immediately after the events, but are remarkable for the masterly criticism of the conduct of the several generals, as well as for the literary ability displayed by the writer.

The following is an extract from a journal which he kept in 1781–1782, and despatched to his father in October, 1782. It was written chiefly by night, 'when,' he says, 'I was almost as much plagued by swarms of troublesome insects flying about the candle and getting into my hair and eyes and under my shirt-collar as I would have been by the enemy.'

. . . . . .

'The newspapers say that a Committee of the House of Commons is appointed to enquire into the causes of Haidar Alí's irruption, and the extent of that calamity. It has extended so far that there is not a human being to be seen in the country—the only inhabitants are the garrisons of the forts, and the British and Mysorean armies.

'The Mysorean army, which encamped before Vellore on the 14th of December [1780], was commanded by Muhammad Alí; Haidar himself remained at Arcot.

'Vellore is situated at the entrance of the Ambúr valley, which leads to one of the principal passes into Mysore, and all convoys coming this way must pass in sight of it; for which reason, a strong guard was always requisite to prevent their being intercepted by the garrison. It was chiefly the dread of this that determined Haidar to attack it. The force that Colonel Lang had to defend it with was two hundred and fifty Europeans and five hundred sepoys, besides a rabble of one thousand two hundred Nawáb's troops and poligars.

'The fortifications were built by the Maráthás more than two hundred years ago. The walls were formed of the same hard stone which had been used at Wandiwash. The stones were three or four feet thick, and eighteen or twenty long, and were placed end-ways. The ditch which surrounded it was two hundred feet broad, and fifteen or twenty deep. Two miles to the right of the fort were three fortified hills. A six-pounder from the nearest threw a shot three hundred yards over the opposite rampart. It was against this that the enemy directed their attack. They began their approaches near a mile from the foot of the wall. Nothing but their numbers could ever have accomplished a work of such amazing labour; the soil on the hills was so thin that they could not make trenches, but were obliged to advance under cover of a wall of gabions, and to fill them they had to bring earth from the plain below. They met many large fragments of rock in their way. They undermined some, and rolled them down the hill; and those they could not manage they avoided by making a sweep round them. In three weeks they had got the better of all these obstacles, and raised a battery, which in a few days demolished one of the angles of the fort. They at the same time raised another on an eminence which overlooked the place; and the garrison, having only a few small guns, could neither return their fire, nor show themselves in the daytime. They laboured hard during the night in cutting off the ruined angle, by a deep trench with a breastwork behind it. On the night of the 10th of January, the enemy, headed by Muhammad Alí in person, made two attacks, and in both were repulsed with great loss.

'It was surprising that Haidar, after raising the siege of Vellore, did not hasten to engage the English army before it was reinforced. Had he been so inclined, he had time enough to have overtaken it, as it lay three days at Wandiwash. Perhaps the high military character of General Coote made him doubtful of success. . . .

'Whilst General Coote carried on this petty war about Cuddalore, Haidar made himself master of Ambúr[1] and Thiagur[2] in the Karnátik: and of all

[1] Ambúr in North Arcot, now a railway station, 112 miles west of Madras. [2] Thiagadrug in South Arcot.

Tanjore but the capital. We must, however, suppose he had good reasons for remaining there. If it was not the smallness of his force, it might have been with a view to keep Haidar to the southward, and to draw his attention from the reinforcement which was then coming from Bengal.

'The General moved in the end of May to raise the siege of Thiagur. He reached Tirivádi the 1st of March [1781], from whence Mír Sáhib retreated on his appearance; here he halted two days, and then returned to his old camp at Cuddalore. I cannot account for this conduct, unless by supposing that from Baillie's defeat he conceived too high an opinion of Haidar's army, and relied too little on his own, or that he did not think the place of sufficient consequence to risk a general engagement to prevent its fall, and that he only moved to divert the enemy and protract the siege.

'The Bengal troops having by this time entered the Karnátik, the General, to hinder Haidar from striking any blow against them, marched to the southward on the 16th June, and two days after arrived at Chilambaram, a fortified pagoda, thirty miles south-west of Cuddalore. Adjoining to the pagoda there is a large pettah, surrounded by a mud wall; the garrison were between two and three thousand poligars. In the evening the General sent three battalions to attack the pettah; the enemy, after a scattered fire, ran to shelter themselves in the pagoda. By some mistake, without orders, the foremost battalion pursued them to the gates; which finding shut, they brought up a twelve-pounder against them. The second shot burst open the outer gate. The sponge staff was fired out of the gun in the hurry, and the man who carried the match was not to be found. In this exigency, Captain Moorhouse of the artillery, with great resolution, loaded and discharged twice, by the help of a musket, and made a breach in the second gate large enough to allow one man to go through at a time. The sepoys rushed in; the space between the two inner gates was in a moment full of them; they did not observe, midway between the two, a flight of steps which led to the rampart. The garrison, every moment dreading the assault, called for quarter, but their voice was not to be distinguished in the general tumult which now ensued. For, some straw having taken fire, caught the clothes of the sepoys, who were crowded between the gateways, and every one pressing back to avoid suffocation and the fire of the enemy (which was now redoubled at the sight of their disaster,) many of them were scorched and burned to death, and those who escaped hurried away without attempting to bring off the twelve-pounder. Six officers and nearly 150 men were killed and wounded in this unfortunate affair.

'The General, who was in the pettah at the time, ordered some pieces of cannon to batter the wall. A fine brass eighteen-pounder was ruined without making any breach; and day beginning to dawn, the troops returned to camp. All thoughts were now relinquished of taking the place by assault; and there being no battering-guns with the army, it was resolved to send for them to Cuddalore; and, after taking the rice out of the pettah, to proceed to Porto Novo to cover their landing. We marched to this place on the 22nd [June], and the same day Mír Sáhib encamped five miles to the westward of it.

'Sir Edward Hughes arrived on the 24th with the battering train; and, whilst rafts were preparing to carry it up the river to Chilambaram, our attention was called to an object of much greater consequence. For, at daybreak on the 28th, the sound of the réveillé was heard in front of the camp, and the rising of the sun discovered to our view the plain for several miles covered with the tents of the Mysorean army. Haidar was preparing to besiege Trichinopoli, when the commandant of Chilambaram advised him of his having repulsed the English, and that they had retreated to Porto Novo. The time he had so long wished for he imagined was now come, when he might, in one day, destroy the only army that remained to oppose him. His expedition showed his confidence of success—he marched seventy miles in two days, and encamped at Mútapolliam, four miles from Porto Novo. His troops were no less sanguine than himself. Some came near enough to the grand guard to warn them of the fate that awaited them so soon as they should come forth to the plain. They bid the foragers, who kept out of reach of the English sentries, not fear them, but go wherever they could find the greatest plenty, for that they would not dare to touch them when they themselves were in the power of Haidar. This language afforded little comfort to the desponding part of our army, who, when they beheld the great extent of the Mysorean camp, and the numerous bodies of horse and foot that moved about it, could not avoid thinking Haidar as formidable as he was represented by those who had escaped from Perambákam, and entertaining the strongest apprehensions of the event of the approaching engagement. But those who considered our artillery, served by men whom Mr. Bellecombe had pronounced superior to everything he had seen in Europe, the perfect discipline of the troops, and their confidence in their commander, regarded Haidar offering battle as the most fortunate circumstance that could have happened.

'A little after daybreak, on the 1st of July, the General drew up the army in a large plain which lay between the two camps. On his right was a chain of sand-hills, which ran along the coast at the distance of about a mile from the sea in the rear; and on the left, woods and enclosures, but with an open space between. Two miles to the left ran another chain of sand-hills, parallel to the former, and behind them lay the principal part of the Mysorean army. At eight o'clock the enemy opened eight guns, in two batteries which they had raised among the sand-banks; but they were too distant to do much execution. The General, having reconnoitred their situation, saw that it was their wish that he should advance across the plain, under the fire of the batteries they had constructed on every side, that their cavalry might be able to take advantage of the impression. He therefore made no change in his disposition, but kept his ground, offering them battle till eleven o'clock, when, finding they did not choose to make the attack, he moved to the rear of the sand-hills on his right. The army marched in two lines, the first commanded by General Munro, the second by General Stuart. In the first were all the European infantry, with six battalions of sepoys equally divided on the flanks; in the second, four battalions of sepoys. One-half of the cavalry formed on the right of the first, the other half on the left of the second line. The baggage, guarded by a regiment of horse and a battalion of sepoys, remained on the beach near Porto Novo. The army, after marching a mile between the sand-banks and the sea-shore, again defiled by an opening into the plain, where the enemy's infantry and artillery were drawn up waiting our coming; but their horse still remained behind the sand-hills.

'In an hour the whole of the first line got into the plain, where they formed under the fire of forty pieces of cannon. Not a shot was returned; the guns were not even unlimbered; but everything remained as if the army had been to continue its march. The enemy, encouraged by this, which they attributed to an intention of escaping, brought their artillery nearer. Every shot now took effect. The General rode along the front, encouraging every one to patience, and reserve their fire till they were ordered to part with it. He only waited accounts from the second line. An aide-de-camp from General Stuart told him that he had taken possession of the sand-hills; he immediately gave orders to advance, and to open all the guns. The artillerymen, who had been so long restrained, now exerted themselves. Their fire was so heavy that nothing could stand before it. The Mysorean infantry only stayed to give one discharge; the drivers hurried away the cannon, while the horse attempted to charge; but they were always broken before they reached the line. In a quarter of an hour the whole were dispersed.

'While the first line were engaged with Haidar, the second was attacked by Tipú and Lally, who were repulsed by General Stuart in all their attacks to drive him from the sand-hills; and when Haidar fled, they followed him. A deep watercourse saved the enemy from pursuit, for we were six hours in crossing it, which they, from the number and goodness of their cattle, had done in one. Our army was 7,500 fighting men. The force of the enemy has been variously estimated. A Portuguese captain, who deserted to us during the action, and who pretended to have seen the returns, made it amount to 300,000 or 400,000 (sic), (I do not remember which; it makes little difference) men that could fight. However it may be, it is certain that their numbers were such that the most exact discipline never could have brought the whole into action.

'I am sure you will be tired before you get to the end of this long story; but I have been particular, because it was this action that first gave a turn to our affairs in the Karnátik, and because it was considered at the time as the most critical battle[1] that had been for a long time fought in India. For what could be a more serious matter than to engage an enemy so superior in numbers, whose great strength in horse enabled him to take every advantage, and when there was no alternative between victory and entire ruin? Had we been once broken, it would have been impossible ever to have rallied when surrounded by such a multitude of cavalry. It was known afterwards that when the action began Haidar issued an order to take no prisoners.'

Haidar Alí died in December, 1782. 'His son Tipú,' writes Munro, 'succeeded to his power without any of those violences so common in Indian governments. He soon afterwards took the field, joined by a considerable body of French, and prepared to besiege Wandiwash.' Early in 1783 the English destroyed the fortifications of Wandiwash and provisioned Vellore; but meantime Tipú had withdrawn, marching off to his own country on hearing of the progress of General Mathews on the Malabar coast. In July Munro was present at the battle of Cuddalore, when the French under M. Bussy were defeated by General Stuart. Munro acted as aide-de-camp to the field-officer of the day, and in concluding his account of

[1] The battle of Porto Novo, July 1, 1781.

the battle he observes, 'There seemed no connexion in our movements; every one was at a loss what to do, and nothing saved our army from a total defeat but the French being, like ourselves, without a general.' News of the peace in Europe, after the treaty of Versailles, led to a cessation of hostilities with the French[1]; and the war in the Karnátik was brought to a close by the treaty with Tipú in March, 1784.

The next few years of Munro's service were uneventful. He, however, saw a good deal of the Madras Presidency, being quartered successively in Madura, Tanjore, Fort St. George, Kásimkota near Vizagapatam, and at Vellore. During these years Munro spent his leisure in the study of Hindustaní and Persian and the literature of those languages. Of Persian he seems to have been a great reader; and a letter of his to a friend in Glasgow about the beginning of 1787 contains not only some interesting criticisms on Persian writers, but a translation of the story of Shylock, which he says he found in a Persian manuscript. This translation was published a few years after in Malone's edition of Shakespeare in the notes to the *Merchant of Venice*, with the remark that 'in a Persian manuscript in the possession of Ensign Thomas Munro of the first battalion of Sepoys, now at

[1] 'The suspension of arms was most unfortunate for the French. The army of Stuart before Cuddalore represented the last hope of the English in Southern India. An attack of the French in force could scarcely have failed to annihilate it. With its destruction Madras and all Southern India would have passed over to the French.' Malleson's *Final French Struggles in India*, p. 74.

Tanjore, is found the following story of a Jew and a Musalmán; the translation was made by Mr. Munro, and kindly communicated to me by Daniel Braithwaite, Esq.'

In August, 1788, Munro, now a lieutenant, was appointed an assistant in the Intelligence Department, under Captain Read, and was attached to the headquarters of the force sent to take possession of the province of Guntúr ceded by the Nizám of the Deccan. 'The most important public transaction,' he says in a letter to his father in January, 1789, 'since my last, is the surrender of the Guntúr Circár to the Company, by which it became possessed of the whole coast from Jagannáth to Cape Comorin.'

Of this important event, by which the annexation of the Districts now known as Kistná, Godávarí, Vizagapatam, and Ganjám—or the Northern Circárs—was completed, he wrote the following account, and gives expression to his opinion on the policy by which it was effected.

'The Nizám made himself master of that province soon after Haidar's invasion of the Karnátik, as an equivalent for the arrears of peshcush [tribute] due to him by the Company for the other Circárs. The Company not being at that time in a situation to compel him to restore it, he kept it quietly for several years; and though Sir John Macpherson sent Mr. Johnson to Haidarábád to demand the restitution of it, he paid little attention to his request. But the Company, seeing their affairs again in a respectable situation, determined to compel him to deliver what they considered as their own property. They ordered Lord Cornwallis to intimate to him that they were willing to discharge their arrears of peshcush, and to pay it regularly in future, but that the restoration of Guntúr must be the price; and that, in case of refusal or delay, their troops would enter the province in fourteen days.

'Colonel Edington, with a detachment of a regiment of Europeans and four battalions of sepoys, being already arrived on the boundary of the Company's territory, on the 9th of September [1788], Captain Kennaway, from Calcutta, presented to the Nizám a paper, containing a demand of the surrender of the Circár, a promise of a faithful discharge of all arrears, as well as regular payment hereafter, and notifying the time limited for the advance of the Company's troops. The Nizám, unable singly to contend with such an antagonist, and despairing of assistance from any of the country powers, (for Tipú was unwilling to make any movement without the co-operation of France, and the Maráthás were employed in expelling a usurper, and reinstating Sháh Alam on the throne of Delhi,) submitted to the terms imposed upon him. He instantly issued orders for his forces to evacuate Guntúr, but, at the same time, protested against the violence and injustice of the Company. "They ought," he said, "to have paid their arrears previous to their insisting on the restoration of the country;—and what security have I," he asked, "that they will be more punctual in future in discharging their peshcush than they have hitherto been?"

'It would certainly have been a more honourable and manly policy to have paid him, first, all his just claims, and then to have made the requisition. The consequence would have been the same, with this difference, that adopting this method would have raised, while following the other has degraded, the name of Englishmen!

'The spirit of the nation humbled in the West by an unfortunate war, seems to have extended its effects to this country, in stooping to a timid, where a bold policy would have been equally safe. The apprehension, if any existed, was groundless, that the Nizám, if he had received the money, might have employed it against the Company, and refused to give up the province. The sum did not amount to the quarter of one year's revenue; and had it been ten times more, it would have availed little; for to a weak and distracted government, without an army, *money* is but a poor defence against a warlike and powerful enemy. He knew that resistance would be in vain, and that it would serve no other purpose than to afford the Company a pretence for withholding the peshcush of the other provinces. He was too wise to give them such an opening, and was no doubt happy to save, in some measure, his credit, by the consideration that they had some claim to the possession of Guntúr. His reply to Captain Kennaway's demand is sensible and candid,—it is the language of a prince, who feels that he is insulted without having the power to avenge himself. The perusal of it is affecting—it displays the humiliation of a great prince compelled to sacrifice his dignity to necessity, and to suppress his indignation at being told that this is done with his own approbation, and purely from motives of friendship, by the English. If I can get a sight of the original, and a few spare hours, I shall send you a translation of it.'

But Munro was a student and critic not only of what was going on about him in India, but of contemporary history and politics in Europe, and his remarks and views on the events then happening may still be read with interest. In a letter to his friend Foulis, from Ambúr in April, 1790, he writes as follows of the likelihood of France becoming a successful rival to Great Britain, and even wresting from her all her foreign possessions:—

'If, like you, I were liable to be possessed by blue or any other devils, the situation of affairs in France would be more likely than anything besides to produce such an event; for as a friend to the glory and prosperity of Britain, I cannot behold with indifference the restoration of French liberty. That nation, already too powerful, wanted nothing but a better form of government to render her the arbiter of Europe; and the convulsions attending so remarkable a revolution having subsided, France will soon assume that rank to which she is entitled from her resources, and the enterprising genius of her inhabitants. You and I may live to see the day when the fairest provinces of India (reversing Mr. Gibbon's boast) shall not be subject to a company of merchants of a remote island in the Northern Ocean; but when, perhaps, those merchants and their countrymen, being confined by the superior power of their rival to the narrow limits of their native isle, shall sink into the insignificance from which they were raised by the empire of the sea. With the freedom of our Government we may retain our orators, our poets, and historians, but our domestic transactions will afford few splendid materials for the exercise of genius or fancy, and with the loss of empire we must relinquish, however reluctantly, the idea so long and so fondly cherished by us all, of our holding the balance of power.

'In looking forward to the rising grandeur of France, I am not influenced by any groundless despondency, but I judge of the future from the past. And when I consider that after the Revolution she opposed for some time, successfully, the united naval powers of England and Holland; that she did the same under Queen Anne, and under George II till 1759; and that notwithstanding the almost total annihilation of her marine in that war—in the East, in Europe, America, and the West Indies—she never shunned, and sometimes sought our fleets, and met us in this country (the East Indies), if not with superior force, at least with superior fortune, and perhaps bravery; that she made all those exertions when she was left to the mercy of capricious women, who made and unmade ministers, generals, and admirals almost every month, and when commerce and even the naval profession met with no encouragement; I cannot but fear that when she shall direct her attention to the sea, she may wrest from Britain her empire of that element, and strip her of all her foreign possessions. When two countries have made nearly the same progress in the arts of peace and war, and when there is no material difference in the constitution of their governments, that which possesses the greatest population, and the most numerous resources from the fertility of her soil, must in the end prevail over her rival. But let us leave this struggle with France, which I hope is yet at some distance, and talk of the affair which we have now upon our hands with Tipú, &c.'

Turning now from Munro's descriptions of campaigns and views on the politics of the day, we have the following graphic account of his daily life as a subaltern in India, and of the hardships and actual poverty he had to endure. The following is from a letter to his sister, dated Madras, January 23, 1789.

'I have often wished that you were transported for a few hours to my room, to be cured of your Western notions of Eastern luxury, to witness the forlorn condition of old bachelor Indian officers; and to give them also some comfort in a consolatory fragment. You seem to think that they live like those satraps that you have read of in plays; and that I in particular hold my state in prodigious splendour and magnificence—that I never go abroad unless upon an elephant, surrounded with a crowd of slaves—that I am arrayed in silken robes, and that most of my time is spent in reclining on a sofa, listening to soft music, while I am fanned by my officious pages; or in dreaming, like Richard, under a canopy of state.

'But while you rejoice in my imaginary greatness, I am most likely stretched on a mat, instead of my real couch; and walking in an old coat, and a ragged shirt, in the noonday sun, instead of looking down from my elephant, invested in my royal garments. You may not believe me when I tell you, that I never experienced hunger or thirst, fatigue or poverty, till I came to India—that since then, I have frequently met with the first three, and that the last has been my constant companion. If you wish for proofs, here they are. I was three years in India before I was master of any other pillow than a book or a cartridge-pouch; my bed was a piece of canvas, stretched on four cross-sticks, whose only ornament was the great-coat that I brought from England, which, by a lucky invention, I turned into a blanket in the cold weather, by thrusting my legs into the sleeves, and drawing the skirts over my head. In this situation I lay, like Falstaff in the basket—hilt to point—and very comfortable, I assure you, all but my feet. For the tailor, not having foreseen the various uses to which this piece of dress might be applied, had cut the cloth so short, that I never could, with all my ingenuity, bring both ends under cover. Whatever I gained by drawing up my legs, I lost by exposing my neck; and I generally chose rather to cool my heels than my head. This bed served me till Alexander went last to Bengal, when he gave me an Europe camp-couch. On this great occasion I bought a pillow and a carpet to lay under me, but the unfortunate curtains were condemned to make pillow-cases and towels; and now, for the first time in India, I laid my head on a pillow.

'But this was too much good fortune to bear with moderation. I began to grow proud, and resolved to live in great style! For this purpose I bought two table-spoons, and two tea-spoons, and another chair—for I had but one before—a table, and two table-cloths. But my prosperity was of short duration, for, in less than three months, I lost three of my spoons, and one of my chairs was broken by one of John Napier's companions. This great blow reduced me to my original obscurity, from which all my attempts to emerge have hitherto proved in vain.

'My dress has not been more splendid than my furniture. I have never been able to keep it all of a piece; it grows tattered in one quarter, while I am establishing funds to repair it in another; and my coat is in danger of losing the sleeves, while I am pulling it off to try on a new waistcoat.

'My travelling expeditions have never been performed with much grandeur or ease. My only conveyance is an old horse, who is now so weak, that, in all my journeys, I am always obliged to walk two-thirds of the way; and if he were to die, I would give my kingdom for another, and find nobody to accept of my offer. Till I came here, I hardly knew what walking was. I have often walked from sunrise to sunset, without any other refreshment than a drink of water; and I have traversed on foot, in different directions, almost every part of the country between Vizagapatam and Madura, a distance of eight hundred miles.

'My house at Vellore consists of a hall and a bed-room. The former contains but one piece of furniture—a table; but on entering the latter, you would see me at my writing-table, seated on my only chair, with the old couch behind me, adorned with a carpet and pillow; on my right hand a chest of books, and on my left two trunks; one for holding about a dozen changes of linen, and the other about half a dozen of plates, knives and forks, &c. This stock will be augmented on my return by a great acquisition, which I have made here—six tea-spoons and a pair of candlesticks, bought at the sale of the furniture of a family going to Europe. I generally dine at home about three times in a month, and then my house looks very superb; every person on this occasion bringing his own chair and plate.

'As I have already told you that I am not Aladdin with the wonderful lamp, and that, therefore, I keep neither pages, nor musicians, nor elephants, you may perhaps, after having had so particular an account of my possessions, wish to know in what manner I pass my leisure hours. How this was done some years ago I scarcely remember; but for the last two years that I have been at Vellore I could relate the manner in which almost every hour was employed.

'Seven was our breakfast-hour, immediately after which I walked out, generally alone; and, though ten was my usual hour of returning, I often wandered about the fields till one. But when I adhered to the rules I had laid down for myself, I came home at ten, and read Persian till one, when I dressed and went to dinner. Came back before three; sometimes slept half an hour, sometimes not, and then wrote or talked Persian and Moors till sunset, when I went to the parade, from whence I set out with a party to visit the ladies, or to play cards at the commanding-officer's. This engaged me till nine, when I went to supper, or more frequently returned home without it, and read politics and nonsense till bed-time, which, according to the entertainment which I met with, happened sometime between eleven and two. I should have mentioned fives as an amusement that occupied a great deal of my time. I seldom missed above two days in a week at this game, and always played two or three hours at a time, which were taken from my walks and Persian studies. Men are much more boyish in this country than in Europe, and, in spite of the sun, take, I believe, more exercise, and are, however strange it may appear, better able to undergo fatigue, unless on some remarkably hot days. I never could make half the violent exertions at home that

I have made here. My daily walks were usually from four to twelve miles, which I thought a good journey in Scotland. You see children of five or six years of age following the camp, and marching fifteen or sixteen miles a day with the same ease as their fathers.

'I have almost as much local attachment to Vellore as to Northside; for it is situated in a delightful valley, containing all the varieties of meadows, groves, and rice-fields. On every side you see romantic hills, some near, some distant, continually assuming new forms as you advance or retire. All around you is classic ground in the history of this country; for almost every spot has been the residence of some powerful family, now reduced to misery by frequent revolutions, or the scene of some important action in former wars.

'Not with more veneration should I visit the field of Marathon, or the Capitol of the ancient Romans, than I tread on this hallowed ground. For, in sitting under a tree, and while listening to the disastrous tale of some noble Moorman, who relates to you the ruin of his fortune and his family, to contemplate by what strange vicissitudes you and he, who are both originally from the North of Asia, after a separation of so many ages, coming from the most opposite quarters, again meet in Hindustán to contend with each other—this is to me wonderfully solemn and affecting.'

Yet, while suffering such privations as he has thus

so graphically described, and while, as he puts it, 'poverty was his constant companion,' Munro and his brother Alexander, also in India, made up between them £100 a year which they regularly remitted to their father, who from a state of affluence had fallen into greater distress than when they left home, and was now with his family mainly dependent on his sons' help. The letters already quoted have shown what a master of style Munro was, whether in narrative, description, or banter. But for tenderness and beauty few published letters could equal those which he wrote to his mother, such as that on the death of one of his brothers, or the following, in which at a previous date he refers to his father's affairs and his efforts to help him:—

'Though my situation is not such as I might have expected, had Sir Eyre Coote lived, yet I still look forward with hope, and do not despair of seeing it bettered. The only cause I have for repining, is my inability to assist my father as I wish, and the hearing that your spirits are so much affected by the loss of his fortune. Yet I cannot but think that you have many reasons for rejoicing. None of your children have been taken from you; and though they cannot put you in a state of affluence, they can place you beyond the reach of want. The time will come, I hope, when they will be able to do more, and to make the latter days of your life as happy as the first. When I compare your situation with that of most mothers whom I remember, I think that you have as little reason for grieving as any of them. Many that are rich, are unhappy in their families. The loss of fortune is but a partial evil; you are in no danger of experiencing the much heavier one—of having unthankful children. The friends that deserted you with your fortune were unworthy of your society; those that deserved your friendship have not forsaken you.

'Alexander and I have agreed to remit my father £100 a year between us. If the arrears which Lord Macartney detained are paid, I will send £200 in the course of the year 1786. John Napier will tell you the reason why it was not in my power to send more.'

CHAPTER III

WAR WITH TIPÚ

THE second Mysore War, or the war with Tipú Sultán, 1790–1792, was brought about by Tipú's invasion of Travancore. The Dutch having sold the fort of Cranganore to the Rájá of Travancore, Tipú asserted that the Rájá of Cochin, being his vassal, had no right to sell it to the Dutch, nor they to another power. The British East India Company then informed him that their ally, the Rájá of Travancore, was much alarmed at his assembling an army on his frontiers. Tipú replied that nothing was further from his thoughts than war. But as soon as he had suppressed a rebellion among the Náirs in Malabar, he passed into Travancore, and, though repulsed at first, soon succeeded in storming the Travancore lines[1]. This was immediately followed by a declaration of war by the British. Hitherto the policy had been to regard Tipú as a useful buffer against the Maráthás, but on his invasion of Travancore a triple alliance was formed against him by the Company, the Maráthás, and the Nizám. A few weeks before the declaration

[1] Fortified barriers erected by the Rájás of Cochin and Travancore about 1775; see Wilks' *History of Mysore*, iii. 31–34.

of war, Munro, then stationed at Ambúr, in writing to his father, January 17, 1790, gave his opinion on the state of affairs and his reasons for differing from the line of policy pursued as regards Tipú. There is, however, space for only a few extracts from this interesting letter.

'It will require some time to assemble an army able to face the enemy; and before such an army can be put in motion, Tipú may be in actual possession of Travancore and all the southern countries. We have derived but little benefit from experience and misfortune. The year 1790 now sees us as unprepared as the year 1780 did for war. We have added to the numbers of our army, but not to its strength, by bringing so many regiments from Europe. For so great a number of Europeans serve only to retard the operations of an Indian army, less by their inability to endure the fatigues of the field, than by the great quantity of cattle which is requisite to convey their provisions and equipage. No addition has been made to our sepoys, on whom we have long depended, and may still with security depend, for the preservation of our empire in this country. We have, therefore, made our army more expensive and numerous, though less calculated for the purposes of war, than formerly, both on account of the multitude of Europeans and the want of cattle. We keep up, it is true, a small establishment of bullocks, but hardly sufficient to draw the guns, far less to transport the prodigious quantity of stores and provisions which follow an army. Had half the money, idly thrown away in sending a naval squadron and four additional regiments to this country, been employed in increasing the establishment of sepoys and cattle, we should then have had an army which, for its lightness and capacity for action, would have broken the power of our formidable rival.

'Exclusive of the unwieldiness of our army, we shall commence the war under the disadvantage of a want of magazines, for we have none at present but at Madras. Since the conclusion of the late war, we have acted as if we had been to enjoy a perpetual peace. . . .

'It has long been admitted as an axiom in politics, by the directors of our affairs, both at home and in this country, that Tipú ought to be preserved as a barrier between us and the Maráthás. This notion seems to have been at first adopted without much knowledge of the subject, and to have been followed without much consideration. It is to support a powerful and ambitious enemy, to defend us from a weak one. From the neighbourhood of the one, we have everything to apprehend; from that of the other, nothing. This will be clearly understood by reflecting for a moment on the different constitutions of the two governments. The one, the most simple and despotic monarchy in the world, in which every department, civil and military, possesses the regularity and system communicated to it by the genius of Haidar, and in which all pretensions derived from high birth being discouraged, all independent chiefs and zamindárs subjected or extirpated, justice severely and impartially administered to every class of people, a numerous and well-disciplined army kept up, and almost every employment of trust or consequence conferred on men raised from obscurity, gives to the government a vigour hitherto unexampled in India. The other, composed of a confederacy of independent chiefs, possessing extensive dominions and numerous armies, now acting in concert, now jealous of each other, and acting only for their own advantage, and at all times liable to be detached from the public cause by the most distant prospect of private gain, can never be a very dangerous enemy to the English. The first is a government of conquest; the last, merely of plunder and depredation. The character of vigour has been so strongly impressed on the Mysore government by the abilities of its founders, that it may retain it, even under the reign of a weak prince, or a minor; but the strength of the supreme Maráthá government is continually varying, according to the disposition of its different members, who sometimes strengthen it by union, and sometimes weaken it by defection, or by dividing their territories among their children.

'That nation likewise maintains no standing army, adopts none of the European modes of discipline, and is impelled by no religious tenets to attempt the extirpation of men of a different belief. But Tipú supports an army of 110,000 men, a large body of which is composed of slaves, called chelas, trained on the plan of the Turkish janizaries, and follows with the greatest eagerness every principle of European tactics. He has even gone so far as to publish a book for the use of his officers, a copy of which is now in my possession, containing, besides the evolutions and manœuvres usually practised in Europe, some of his own invention, together with directions for marching, encamping, and fighting; and he is, with all his extraordinary talents, a furious zealot in a faith which founds eternal happiness on the destruction of other sects.

'An opportunity for humbling an enemy so dangerous, and so implacable, has now appeared; and had we been in the state of readiness for action which good policy demanded of us, one army might have entered the Coimbatore country and another sat down before Bangalore, almost before he could have opposed us. But so far from this, no army is yet likely to assemble; and it was with much difficulty that Colonel Musgrave prevailed on the Governor to send the 36th regiment, two battalions of sepoys, one regiment of cavalry, and a company of artillery, to Trichinopoli. But the troops there, even when joined by this detachment, will not form an army that will be able to act offensively.

'Our operations will be still farther impeded by the reference which it will, most likely, be judged expedient to make to Bengal, before we proceed on an offensive war. The public look impatiently for the arrival of ——[1], and seem to be sanguine in their

[1] Probably Lord Cornwallis is referred to.

expectations of the happy effects to be derived from the ability and exertions of so distinguished a character. Experience might have taught them, at least in this country, to build less on great names; for they have seen so many impositions on the understanding of mankind, invested with high offices, and recommended by common fame, as were enough to prejudice them against any man who should come among them with such credentials.'

Throughout the war with Tipú, Lieut. Munro was actively engaged, and in his Memorandum of Services he specifies the various engagements and duties in which he took part. He was in command of a body of sepoys called the Prize Guard, was present when the fort of Bangalore was taken by storm, was at the battle of Karigal, at the siege of Seringapatam, and after the peace in March, 1792, he marched with the detachment in charge of the two sons of Tipú who were sent as hostages to Madras.

In long letters to his father, Munro describes the events of the war, and with minute detail the operations of the British troops at Pálghát, in Malabar, and at Satyamangálam, Erode, Karúr, Dhárapuram, and Coimbatore, all in the Coimbatore District; and at Tirupatúr, Krishnagiri, and Káveripatam in the Salem District. Commenting on the two days' fighting with Tipú at Satyamangálam he observes: 'There seems to be a fatality sometimes attending the greatest geniuses, which deadens the energy of their minds, and reduces them to the level of common men, at the moment when their best concerted schemes are going to be crowned with success. Had Tipú acted with more decision on September 14, by bringing up more guns and pressing Floyd closer, he would probably have defeated him; or, if not that day, he would undoubtedly have done it the following; for not a man of the detachment had eaten or slept for two days, and they could have made little resistance to another attack. The General, who had gone by mistake, for it would be unjust to impute it to design, towards Dhannáyakankóta, could not have been near to support them; and after their defeat, he would himself have fallen an easy sacrifice, for he had only three battalions of sepoys, and two of Europeans, without their flank companies; and even Colonel Stuart would have been fortunate had he escaped with his detachment from Pálghát. The Colonel was so much convinced that these things would take place, that, on receiving information from the General of Floyd's situation, he made preparations for retreating (on the first accounts of the loss of the army, which he expected every moment to learn) with all his force to Cochin. Tipú, fortunately for us, did not act with his usual vigour, and the southern army escaped from destruction.'

Munro's relations, naturally proud of his graphic accounts of the war with Tipú, published one of his letters in a London paper. On hearing of this he destroyed what he calls a long treatise on the war.

'There was no use in keeping it,' he writes, 'when I could not venture to send it to those for whose amusement it was intended. It mentioned what ought to have been the general plan of the war; explained the impolicy of commencing it in Coimbatore, which I believe I took notice of before General Medows joined the army; the propriety of advancing from the Karnátik to Bangalore; pointed out the mistake of the Seringapatam expedition as well as the manner in which it ought to be next attempted and the government of Tipú entirely overthrown; and by a discussion of the nature of Maráthá armies, their method of marching, and the way of supplying them with provisions, showed how little cause there was of apprehension from them.'

The details he gives of the siege of Bangalore and of the subsequent operations are published in Gleig's *Life*, and are well worth reading, but are too long to quote here. So also are the letters he wrote when the idea was entertained of a speedy accommodation with Tipú. Against this he argued strongly, and derided the policy of maintaining in India the balance of power. 'Men read books,' he wrote, 'and because they find that all warlike nations have had their downfall, they declaim against conquest as not only dangerous but unprofitable, from a supposition that the increase of territory must be always followed by a proportionable increase of expense. This may be true when a nation is surrounded by warlike neighbours, which, while it gains a province on one side, loses as much on the other. But there are times and situations where conquest not only brings a revenue greatly beyond its expenses, but brings also additional security. The kings of England knew this when they attempted the reduction of Scotland. There is, however, another example which would apply better to our position in the Karnátik. When Spain was, in the last century, engaged in a war with France and Portugal, would not the possession of the latter country have added much to her strength and security, by removing every possibility of attack from the frontiers of France? By subduing the country below the Ghâts, from Palgatcherry to Ambúr, we have nothing to fear. The sea is behind us, and in front we gain a stronger barrier than we now have, which would enable us to defend the country with the present military establishment; but as this, with the civil expenses, would be nearly equal to the whole revenue of the country, let us advance to the Kistna, and we shall triple our revenue without having occasion to add much to our military force; because our barrier will then be both stronger and shorter than it is now.'

In the following letter, dated April 28, 1792, Munro criticizes the negotiations with Tipú and the terms of the peace that were entered into. Subsequent events showed how correct was his view of the situation and his foresight as to the steps that should have been taken to prevent a recurrence of hostilities on the part of Tipú.

'I am so little pleased with the peace, that I cannot without difficulty bring myself either to talk or write of it. When hostilities ceased, Tipú had no place above the Gháts from Gurramkonda to Seringapatam. Besides the former of these forts, he had Gooty, Bellary, and Chitaldrúg; but all either so distant from the scene of action, or so weakly garrisoned, as to give him no benefit from holding them. He had likewise Krishnagiri, in the Bárámahal, which was, however, at this time, of no consequence in the operations of the war, because its garrison was not strong enough to attack convoys coming from the Karnátik, and because the Peddanaididurgum Pass, in the neighbourhood of Ambúr, being repaired, all convoys, after the month of September, took that road as the most direct to the army. He had lost the greatest part of his troops by death or desertion in the attack of his lines, and he himself had lost his haughtiness, his courage, and almost every quality that distinguished him, but his cruelty, which he continued to exercise every day on many of the principal officers of his government, particularly Bráhmans, on the most idle suspicions. The remains of his infantry were in the fort, and his cavalry on the glacis. He slept at night in the fort, in the great mosque,—for he never visited his palace after his defeat on the 6th; and during the day he stayed on the outside amongst his horsemen, under a private tent, from whence he observed, with a sullen despair, his enemies closing in upon him from every side—the

Karnátik army, on the north bank of the river, with their approaches, which even on this side were carried within four thousand yards of the wall, and a strong detachment occupying the pettah, and half the island—the Bombay army on the south side, about four miles distant, on the Periyapátná road—Parasu Rám Bháo, after ravaging Biddanore, advancing by rapid marches to fill up the interval between the right of the Bombay and the left of the Karnátik army, and complete the blockade—and no possibility of protracting the siege, even by the most determined resistance, beyond fifteen days. In this situation, when extirpation, which had been so long talked of, seemed to be so near, the moderation or the policy of Lord Cornwallis granted him peace, on the easy terms of his relinquishing half his dominions to the confederates. Tipú accepted these conditions on the 24th of February, and orders were instantly issued to stop all working in the trenches. The words which spread such a gloom over the army, by disappointing not so much their hopes of gain as of revenge, were these: "Lord Cornwallis has great pleasure in announcing to the army that preliminaries of peace have been settled between the Confederate Powers and Tipú Sultán."

'His Lordship probably at this time supposed that everything would soon be finally settled, and that he would be able in a few days to leave a sickly camp, where he was losing great numbers of Europeans; but Tipú continued to work with more vigour than before the cessation, and used so many delays and evasions in ratifying the definitive treaty, that notwithstanding his having already sent his two eldest sons as hostages, and a million sterling, it was believed that hostilities would be renewed. His Lordship furnished him with the means of protraction by adopting a revenue instead of a geographical division of his country. It was stipulated that the confederates were to take portions of his territories contiguous to their own, and by their own choice, which should amount to half his revenue. He was desired to send out an account of his revenues, that the selection might be made. He replied that he had none—that they had all been lost at Bangalore and other places; and on being told that in that case the allies would make the partition agreeable to statements in their own possession, he sent out accounts in which the frontier countries were overrated, and all those in the centre of his kingdom, which he knew he would retain for himself, undervalued. The fabrication was obvious, not only in this particular, but also in his diminishing the total amount of his revenue about thirty lacs of rupees. The confederates, however, after a few days, consented to submit to this double loss for the sake of peace; but Tipú, after gaining one point, determined to try his success on some others. The value of the whole had been fixed; but on proceeding to fix that of the districts which were to be ceded, he threw so many obstacles in the way, that the allies found themselves at last compelled to adopt the measure with which they ought to have begun. A list was sent to him, which he was told contained half his dominions, and he was desired to put his seal to it. After a delay of two days, he replied that he would neither give up Krishnagiri, Chitaldrúg, nor Gooty. His unwillingness to part with these places, which could only be useful to him in an offensive war, convinced his Lordship of his hostile designs, and made him resolve to insist on their being surrendered: he ordered parties to make fascines, and the young princes to go next morning to Bangalore. The vakils of Tipú, seeing his sons marching off at daybreak, ran and called up Sir John Kennaway, and begged that they might be detained till they should inform the Sultán, and get *another* final answer from him. His Lordship, with his usual mildness, permitted them to halt after they had proceeded about two miles; but still it was not till the 16th, three days afterwards, that the vakils signed the treaty; and it did not come out till the 19th with the signature of Tipú.

'So much good sense and military skill has been shown in the conduct of the war, that I have little doubt but that the peace has been made with equal judgment. It has given us an increase of revenue amounting to thirty-nine and a half lacs of rupees, which, though from Tipú's mismanagement of his finances it has not produced that for some years past, will soon be easily afforded by the country; and by giving us possession of the Bárámahal, it has rendered it extremely difficult, if not impossible, for Tipú to invade the Karnátik in future from the westward,—for the passes from Mysore into the Bárámahal, though good, are few; and though not defended by fortifications, there are so many strong posts near them, that an invading army must either take them, which might require a whole campaign, or else leave them in the rear, and run the risk of being starved by the loss of its convoys. These are, no doubt, great advantages; but because greater might have been with ease obtained, I cannot help thinking but that something has been left undone. Why, instead of stumbling upon revenue accounts, could we not have traced our boundary on the map, taken such places as suited us from their political situation, sent him entirely above the Ghâts, and not left him in possession of Karúr and Coimbatore, to plunder our southern provinces whenever he shall find it convenient to go to war?

'It is true, that the possession of Palgatcherry will make it always easy for a Bombay army to take Coimbatore, and force him above the Ghâts, with the assistance of a Karnâtik army; but to collect our troops is a work of some months, and in that time he may pass Trichinopoli, and ravage the Karnâtik as far as Madras; whilst, by driving off the cattle and inhabitants, he may render it difficult for us to equip an army for the field. If we are in a situation to march, he will probably lose Bangalore in the first campaign. But he will always be able to prevent an army without cavalry from besieging Seringapatam; and while he can do this, he can force us, after an expensive war, to relinquish our conquests for peace. We ought, therefore, to have kept Coimbatore, and established a strong post at Satyamangálam, which would have made an invasion on that side as impracticable as on that of the Bárámahal. Tipú being then without magazines in the low countries, and seeing strong posts in the neighbourhood of all the passes, which could defy his unskilful attacks and intercept his convoys, would have had no temptation to begin a hopeless war; but as the allies must also have had a proportional increase of territory, it is said that he would then have been reduced too low. He would have been more powerful than Haidar was when he usurped the government, and would have been as able as he to defend his possessions; and if he was not, so much the better. For every person who has seen his army, and that of the other country powers, must be convinced how much is to be feared from the one, and how little from the other.

'Lord Cornwallis was apprehensive that he should have been driven to the necessity of taking Seringapatam; and frequently exclaimed, "Good God! what shall I do with this place?" I would have said, "Keep it as the best barrier you can have to your own countries; and be confident that, with it, and such a frontier as the Káveri, skirted by vast ranges of rugged mountains, which make it impassable for an army from Arakere to Káveripuram, no Indian power will ever venture to attack you." But everything now is done by moderation and conciliation;—at this rate, we shall be all Quakers in twenty years more. I am still of the old doctrine, that the best method of making all princes keep the peace, not excepting even Tipú, is to make it dangerous for them to disturb your quiet. This can be done by a good army. We have one; but as we have not money to pay it, we ought to have taken advantage of our successes for this purpose, and after reducing Seringapatam, have retained it and all the countries to the southward and westward of the Káveri. By doing this, we could have maintained a good body of cavalry; and so far from being left with a weak and extended frontier, the usual attendant of conquests, we should, from the nature of the country, have acquired one more compact and more strong than we have at present.

'If peace is so desirable an object, it would be wiser to have retained the power of preserving it in our hands, than to have left it to the caprice of Tipú, who, though he has lost half his revenue, has by no means lost half his power. He requires no combination, like us, of an able military governor, peace in Europe, and allies in this country, to enable him to prosecute war successfully. He only wants to attack them singly when he will be more than a match for any of them; and it will be strange if he does not find an opportunity when the confederates may not find it convenient to support the general cause. When we have a General of less ability than Lord Cornwallis at the head of the Government, (such men as we have lately seen commanding armies,) Tipú may safely try, by the means of Gooty, Chitaldrúg, and Biddanore, to recover the conquests of the Maráthás and the Nizám. If Lord Cornwallis himself could not have reduced Tipú without the assistance of the Maráthás,—for there is no doubt that without them he could never, after falling back from Seringapatam in May, have advanced again beyond Bangalore,—if his integrity, his sound manly judgment, and his great military talents could have done nothing, what is to be hoped for from those whom we may expect to supply his room? We cannot look for better than ——, or ——, or ——, men selected from the army as great military characters. But these gentlemen themselves are as well convinced as any private in the army, how cheap Tipú held them, and how little honour he could have gained by foiling them. One, or rather two, sallied forth; and after spouting some strange, unintelligible stuff, like ancient Pistol, and the ghosts of Romans, lost their magazines by forming them in front of the army, and then spent the remainder of the campaign in running about the country, after what was ludicrously called by the army the invisible power, asking which way the bull ran!

'The other, in May last, on a detachment of Tipú's marching towards him without ever seeing them, with an army superior to Sir Eyre Coote's at Porto Novo, shamefully ran away, leaving his camp and his hospital behind; and in advancing in February, a second time, when Tipú had lost the greatest part of his army, he allowed a few straggling horse to cut off a great part of his camp equipage, and would have lost the whole had not Colonel Floyd been sent with a small detachment to bring him safely past the ferocious Tipú. The Colonel found him as much dismayed as if he had been surrounded by the whole Austrian army, and busy in placing an ambuscade to catch about six looties [1]. He must have been a simple looty that he caught! Lord Cornwallis said one day, on hearing that the looties had carried away nine elephants near Savandrúg, "that they were the best troops in the world, for that they were always doing something to harass their enemies;" and I am confident that Tipú has not lost a looty in his army who is not a better soldier than any of these three Generals. Had his Lordship not arrived, Tipú would have been too much for them all, and their confederates at their back. These characters have led me out of my way, or I should have said a great deal more about the armies of the Native Powers, the old subject of Tipú as a barrier against the Maráthás, and some oversights which his Lordship had nearly committed when he intended sending Medows with a part of the army to Assore to wait for him.'

[1] *Looty*, a plunderer; see Yule's *Hobson-Jobson*.

CHAPTER IV

THE BÁRÁMAHAL—MUNRO AS COLLECTOR

BY the treaty of Seringapatam, Tipú ceded half his dominions to the East India Company and their allies—the Nizám and the Maráthás. The portion that came to the Company was the District of *Malabar* on the west coast, *Dindigal*, now part of the District of Madura, and what was then known as the *Bárámahal*, a part of the present District of Salem.

For the civil administration of the latter of these Lord Cornwallis selected Captain Read, with the title of Superintendent of Revenue of the Bárámahal; and Lieutenant Munro and two other military officers were appointed as his assistants. The selection of military officers for this work was due partly to the deficiency of civil servants with a sufficient knowledge of the language, and partly to the unsatisfactory manner in which the revenue administration of the older possessions of the Company had been conducted. In the Northern Circárs, for example, the land belonged chiefly to zamindárs, who paid a fixed sum to Government, farming out the land to renters, who collected the revenue from the ráyats, and, as might be expected, pillaged them with unauthorized exactions. The renting system was also adopted for collecting the revenue in land not under zamindárs, and in the Jágír [1], with similar results to the ráyats, or cultivators, and with considerable loss to the Government; 'the maladministration,' says Sir Alexander Arbuthnot, 'was intensified by the intervention of a class of persons called "dubashes," some of them domestic servants of the European residents at Madras, who after the invasion of the Karnátik by Haidar in 1780, purchased rights in the land at absurdly low rates, and exercised a most mischievous influence in the district.'

The Bárámahal [2], in which Munro spent the next seven years of his service, 1792–1799, consisted of the Táluks of Krishnagiri, Dharmápuri, Utankarai, and Tirupatúr; these, with Hosúr, which was acquired in 1799, form the most beautiful part of the Salem District, itself perhaps the most picturesque in the Madras Presidency. The area of these Táluks varies from about 600 to 1,200 square miles, with a total of 3,300; the chief town of each is named after it, or the Táluk after the town, but they are all small places, only Tirupatúr having more than 10,000 inhabitants at the present day. The trunk roads, connecting Salem from one direction and Madras from the east with Bangalore, are well made, and in most places are for miles planted on both sides with banian trees, which form

[1] The present District of Chengalput.

[2] *Bárámahal* means the twelve palaces, i. e. the 'tract ruled from the twelve palaces.

a continuous avenue, 'a pillared shade high overarched [1],' affording shelter even in the hottest weather. 'Between Ráyakota and Krishnagiri,' writes Mr. Le Fanu, 'is a winding ghát which is perhaps only second in point of beauty of all the natural beauties of the Salem District. Commencing about half a mile east of Ráyakota, it winds through the verdure-clad hills which abound here; sometimes descending over steep declivities, and again wandering through grassy glades at the bottom of valleys, which echo to the song of birds and abound with all the wealth of tropical growth, while over all the bare peaks, with the durgam as their king, tower in rich shades of grey, brown and even crimson, due to the weathering of the mother rock. Shorter than the road is the track used by foot travellers and known as the Púvatti ghát, which penetrates the thick jungles where the banditti of the country love to lurk; here the footstep startles the hare from its form, and the jungle cock runs clattering to his mates in the bamboo undergrowth, while herds of deer cross the path, and halt to gaze in mute surprise at the trespassers on their favourite haunts [2].'

Not less enthusiastic is Munro's description of Tirupatúr: 'There is nothing to be compared to it in England, nor, what you will think higher praise, in Scotland. It stands in the midst of an extensive fertile valley, from ten to forty miles wide and sixty or seventy long, surrounded by an amphitheatre of mountains of every shape, many of them twice as

[1] *Par. Lost*, ix. 1107. [2] *Salem District Manual*, ii. 251.

high as the Grampians [1]. The country here among the hills has none of the cold and stinted appearance which such countries have at home. The largest trees, the richest soil, and the most luxuriant vegetation, are usually found among naked masses of granite at the bottom of the hills.' Writing of a spot near Dharmápuri where he had made a garden, Munro says that whenever he happened to be at Dharmápuri he always spent at least an hour every day at it, 'and to quit it now goes as much to my heart as forsaking an old friend.' In all these places, in Krishnagiri, in Dharmápuri, at Ráyakota, in the Topúr Pass, at Omalúr, at Sankaridrúg, the bungalows in which Munro lived, the tanks and choultries he had built, and even some of the trees he planted, still remain, so that wherever an official now travels or halts there is something to remind him of Munro. But though nearly a century has passed away since Munro settled the Salem District, it is in the affections of the people, and as the ráyats' friend, that he is best remembered.

The administration of the Báràmahal under both Haidar and Tipú had been oppressive in the extreme; and the first thing that Read and Munro had to do was to settle the amount and the mode of the collection of the revenue, and this was done in such a way as to result in the permanent welfare of the people and benefit to the State. The system adopted was that

[1] The Shevaroy Hills, a well-known sanitarium five miles from Salem, are over 4,500 feet above the sea-level.

which, with some modifications, was afterwards extended over the Madras Presidency, and is known as the Ráyatwárí system. Under it the revenue is collected by the Government officers direct from the ráyats; an annual enquiry is made as to the extent of such holding, as the ráyat has the option to give up, or diminish, or extend his holding from year to year; but there is no annual settlement of the rate of assessment, as is sometimes erroneously supposed. The ráyat under this system is virtually a proprietor with a simple and perfect title, and has all the benefits of a perpetual lease without its responsibility. Every registered holder of land is recognized as its proprietor, and pays the revenue assessed upon his holding direct to Government; he is at liberty to sublet his property or to transfer it by gift, sale, or mortgage; and he cannot be ejected by Government so long as he pays the fixed assessment. In unfavourable seasons remissions are granted for entire or partial loss of produce; the assessment is fixed in money and does not vary from year to year, except where water is drawn from a Government source of irrigation, nor is any addition made to the assessment for improvements effected at the ráyat's own expense; he receives assistance in bad seasons, and cannot be evicted as long as he pays his dues.

In a long letter[1] to Capt. Allen, dated June 8, 1794, Munro describes the revenue system adopted by him in the Bárámahal, contrasting it with Haidar's

[1] Gleig's *Life*, vol. i. pp. 174–180.

system of finance, and describing the nature of the country and its products, and giving his views as to the advisability of the abolition of road duties, taxes on ploughs, houses, trades, cotton, &c. He begins by saying, 'You seem to think that I have a great stock of hidden knowledge of revenue and other matters, which I am unwilling to part with. I have more than once endeavoured to convince you that we have no mysteries, that we have made no new discoveries, and that our only system is *plain hard labour*. Whatever success may have hitherto attended the management of these districts it is to be ascribed to this talent alone, and it must be unremittingly exerted, not so much to make collections as to prevent them, by detecting and punishing the authors of private assessments which are made in almost every village in India. We have only to guard the ráyats from oppression and they will create the revenue for us.'

In a letter to his father from the 'Bank of the Káveri, opposite Erode,' in January, 1795, Munro expostulates with him for endeavouring to obtain promotion for him through a Mr. P., apparently by showing the latter some of his letters. 'They might,' he writes, 'raise the curiosity of Mr. P., but could give him no very favourable opinion of me,' and 'if he took any step in my favour, his doing so would be highly improper, for it is from the reports of Government and the Board of Revenue, under whom I immediately act, and not from my own, that he ought to form his judgment of my fitness for being entrusted with a civil employment.' In this letter he makes the following remarks as to the necessity of collectors knowing the language of the country and being properly paid, and on the system of annual settlement, which had not yet been modified into the ráyatwárí system as described above. He says:—

'Great additions might certainly be made to the Company's revenue on the coast. The first step should be to find proper men to manage it; for, unless this is done, every attempt at improvement will be in vain. No man should get the charge of a district who does not understand the language of the natives; for unless he had perseverance enough for this, he will never have enough for a collector; and he would besides be kept under the dominion of his servants, and ignorant of everything that was passing around him. Government have at least been convinced of the necessity of such a regulation; and Sir Charles Oakeley [1], just before he departed, issued an order that after the 1st of January, 1796, no person would be appointed a collector who did not understand some of the country languages.

'To this knowledge and zeal in fulfilling the duties of their station, collectors should also unite a sound constitution, capable of bearing heat and fatigue; for if they are not active in going about their districts, and seeing everything themselves, the petty officers under them, in combination with the head-farmers, will make away with the revenue on pretence of bad

[1] Governor of Madras, Aug. 1792 to Sept. 1794.

seasons. In this country, where there are so few Europeans, and where all business of taxation is transacted in a strange language, Government have scarcely any means of learning how the collector conducts himself, except from his own reports; and to think of preventing his embezzlements by multiplying official checks, would only be an idle waste of time and money. This evil, which can never be entirely removed, would best be remedied by selecting men of industry and talents, and placing them beyond the necessity of perverting the public money to their private use.

'A collector ought to have at least a thousand pagodas a month; he will probably have been eight or ten years in the country before he receives his appointment; and allowing that he remains ten more, and that he annually spends half his income, which he may do without being very extravagant, by having no fixed place of abode, and keeping an extra number of servants and horses for frequent travelling, he may, at the end of twenty years, return home not much richer than he ought to be. The Revenue Board made some time ago an application for an increase of salary to collectors, which Government rejected, with great marks of displeasure; but, in doing this, they showed little knowledge either of true policy or human nature; for when men are placed in situations where they can never become independent by their avowed emoluments, but where they may also, by robbing the public without any danger of discovery, become so on a sudden, the number of those who would balance which side to take is so small, that it ought not to be brought into the account.

'We see every day collectors, who always lived above their salary, amassing great fortunes in a very few years. The operation by which this is accomplished is very simple:—when rents are paid in money, by giving Government a rent-roll below the real one, and when in kind, by diminishing the produce of the land or of the sales. It is in vain to say that collectors, being men of education and character, will not descend to such practices; the fact is against this conclusion. It is the same thing whether it is done by themselves or by those under them. It may be said, that their gains arise from the successful trade of their agents; but when these very agents are invested with all their authority, and can, by pushing the payment of the rents, and other contrivances, get the whole produce of the lands into their hands at their own price, it is easy to see how dear such a trade costs both Government and the people The immediate deduction, though considerable, is not all the loss that revenue sustains, the obstruction of improvement ought also to be reckoned; for men occupied in such schemes cannot have much leisure to attend to the extension of cultivation. . . .

'The rents in some parts of the Karnátik are regulated by the grain sown, every kind paying a different rate, and in others they are levied in kind; and, in all, the leases are annual. Where the rents are fixed according to the grain, the lands are measured every year. The surveyors, in making their reports, are guided by the bribes they receive, and a thousand frauds are practised both on the farmers and the Government; and where they are collected in kind, the produce of the land is either thrown upon the cultivator, at a price much above its value, or else a standard is fixed for the market, below which no person can sell until the whole of the public grain has been disposed of. Such wretched management, one would think, must soon ruin the country; but the universal custom of early marriages is favourable to population; and the inhabitants, under all their oppressions, seldom quit their native villages, because they are attached to them, and can go nowhere that they will not experience the same treatment. They soon forget their wrongs, for they must live; and they again cultivate their fields the succeeding year, with the certainty of being plundered in the same manner as the last. This insecurity of property, though a great obstacle to the increase of revenue, does not diminish it much; for, as the greatest part of it is at present drawn from grain, the source of it cannot be lessened in any great degree without starving the inhabitants; and they will not want subsistence as long as it can be provided so easily.

'A man has only to furnish himself with a couple of bullocks,—a plough hardly costs a sixpence. If he turns up the soil three or four inches, and scatters his seed, he is sure of a sufficient return. Were we to abandon our present oppressive mode of taxation, the country, instead of rice and dry grain, would be covered with plantations of betel, cocoa-nut, sugar, indigo, and cotton; and the people would take a great deal of our manufactures, for they are remarkably fond of many of them, particularly of scarlet; but, unfortunately, few of them can afford to wear it. Many Bráhmans use a square piece of it as a cloak, during the wet and cold weather; but I don't remember ever seeing any of the farmers with it. When they can appear fine, and think there is no danger in doing so, there is no doubt but that great numbers of them will substitute it for the camly, a coarse thick woollen stuff, with which all of them are provided, which they carry in all seasons to defend themselves from the sun and rain, and on which they sit by day and sleep by night.

'It is a mistaken notion that Indians are too simple in their manners to have any passion for foreign manufactures. In dress, and every kind of dissipation but drinking, they are at least our equals. They are hindered from taking our goods, not by want of inclination, but either by poverty; or the fear of being reputed rich, and having their rents raised. When we relinquish the barbarous system of annual settlements; when we make over the lands, either in very long leases or in perpetuity, to the present occupants; and when we have convinced them, by making no assessments above the fixed rent, for a series of years, that they are actually proprietors of the soil, we shall see a demand for European articles of which we have at present no conception. If we look only to the security of our own power in this country, it would perhaps be wiser to keep the lands, as they now are, in the possession of Government, giving them to the inhabitants in leases of from five to twenty years, than to make them over to them for ever, because there is reason to fear that such a property may beget a spirit of independence, which may one day prove dangerous to our authority; but neither the present revenue, nor any future increase of it, can be depended upon, while our military force is inadequate to the defence of our territories, and while the enemy can ravage them, and drive away the people, without our being able to hinder them. We require for this purpose at least 6,000 or 7,000 cavalry: an invasion would cost us more in six months than the additional expense of such a corps would amount to in ten years.

'While our army is composed only of infantry, our power here will always be in the most critical situation in the time of war; for one defeat may ruin us; because against an enemy strong in horse, defeat and extirpation are the same. He may lose many battles without much injury to his affairs, because we cannot pursue; but by one victory he annihilates our army. It was on this principle that Haidar fought us so often in 1781; and had he once defeated Sir Eyre Coote, he would soon have been master of every place in the Karnátik but Madras. Four or five thousand horse might just now lay waste the Karnátik, and Tipú, by following rapidly with the main body, might make it a very difficult and tedious business for us to collect our scattered army to oppose him. He might, in the meantime, collect and drive off the inhabitants; the communication with his own country would be secured by posting a detachment at Pálákod,—for Krishnagiri, the only place of consequence in the neighbourhood, is above fifteen miles from the great road, and as the garrison is only one battalion, no party could be spared from it to interrupt the march of his convoys. But if we had 6,000 or 7,000 cavalry, such an invasion could not with safety be attempted: irregular horse would not venture alone into the Karnátik; and if they waited till Tipú marched with his infantry, our army might be drawn together in time to oppose him at entering, or at least to overtake him before he could reascend the Gháts. He might be forced to fight, and the loss of a battle, at so great a distance from home, and against an enemy now strong in cavalry, might be attended by the total destruction of his army. There is no way of protecting the country but by such a body of horse; it would be more effectual than a dozen of forts. The revenues of the Karnátik, under proper management, might, in a few years, yield the additional sum that would be required for this establishment.

'It is of the greatest importance to have a well-appointed army, not only to carry us successfully through a war, but also to deter any of our neighbours from attacking us; because, whether beaten or not, they still receive some new instruction in the military art. Though they are averse to innovations, yet the force of example will at last operate on them as well as on other people. Their improved mode of carrying on war is a sufficient proof of this; and if they continue to make such advances as they have done under Haidar, Sindhia, and Tipú, they will, in thirty or forty years, be too powerful for any force that we can oppose to them. It is on this account very absurd policy to keep two battalions with the Nizám, to teach him, or his successor, to fight us. He has already formed above twenty corps on the same model. We have got a strange fancy, that, for the sake of the balance of power, it is necessary to support him against the Maráthás; but we have less to fear from them than from him and Tipú; because the Moors are more ready than the Hindus in adopting the improvements of strangers, and are likewise, by the spirit of their religion, strongly impelled to extend their empire. I am convinced that, were the Maráthás to overturn both the Muhammadan powers, we would be more secure than at present. They would see that nothing was to be gained by attacking us, and would therefore let us remain quiet, and either fight among themselves, or turn their arms to the northward; and when they had only Asiatics to contend with, they would by degrees lose the little of European discipline which they have already learned. I believe I have all this time only been repeating what I have often said to you before.'

In the short compass of this volume it would be almost impossible to give the reader an idea of the charm of style or of the interesting contents of Munro's letters to his family and friends. The details of his daily work, his tours from village to village, his description of the habits of the people, his conversations with them, his references to the books he had been reading, to the topics of the day, the state of the country and of the army, and his views as to what should be done for the consolidation of the British possessions in India, are all most interesting reading, and show a vein of humour and a fund of imagination, coupled with sagacity and foresight, that prove the writer to have been a man of no ordinary intellect, but also far in advance of his time. Where all his correspondence is so entertaining the difficulty is to decide what to omit. The following are extracts from letters written between 1795 and 1798.

'The place where I am now (Dharmápuri) is far from being so pleasant, because, besides being the station of a cutcherry, and a large noisy village, it is on the high road from Krishnagiri to Salem and Sankaridrúg, by which means, though I have many visitors whom I am happy to see, I have sometimes others who are as tedious as any of your forenoon gossips. We have no inns in this country; and as we have much less ceremony than you have at home, it is always expected that a traveller, whether he is known or not, shall stop at any officer's house he finds on the road When a tiresome fellow comes across me, it is not merely a forenoon's visit of which you complain so heavily, but I have him the whole day and night to myself. I do not, however, stand so much upon form as you do with your invaders. I put him into a hut called a room, with a few pamphlets or magazines, and a bundle of Glasgow newspapers, and leave him to go to business, whether I have any or not, till dinner-time, at four in the afternoon; and if I find that his conversation is too oppressive for my constitution to bear, I give him a dish of tea,—for we have no suppers now in this country,—and leave him at seven to go to more business. There is nothing in the world so fatiguing as some of these *tête à têtes*—they have frequently given me a headache in a hot afternoon; and I would rather walk all the time in the sun, than sit listening to a dull fellow, who entertains you with uninteresting stories, or, what is worse, with uninteresting questions. I am perfectly of your way of thinking about visitors. I like to have them either all at once in a mass, or if they come in ones and twos to have them of my own choosing. When they volunteer, I always wish to see two or three of them together, for then you have some relief; but it is a serious business to be obliged to engage them singly. I wonder that we waste so much of our time in praying against battle and murder, which so seldom happen, instead of calling upon Heaven to deliver us from the calamity to which we are daily exposed, of troublesome visitors.'

'If solitude is the mother of wisdom, it is to be hoped that, in a few years more, I shall be as wise as Solomon or Robinson Crusoe. There is another thing in favour of this idea,—the simplicity of my fare, which, according to some philosophers, is a great friend to genius and digestion. I do not know if the case is altered by this diet being the effect of necessity, and not of choice. When my cook brings me a sheep, it is generally so lean that it is no easy matter to cut it. Fowls are still worse, unless fed with particular care,—a science for which I have no turn; and as to river-fish, very few of them are eatable. If the fish and fowl were both boiled, it would puzzle any naturalist to tell the one from the other merely by the taste. Some sects of philosophers recommend nuts and apples, and other sorts of fruit; but nothing is to be found either in the woods or gardens here, except a few limes, and a coarse kind of plantain, which is never eaten without the help of cookery. I have dined to-day on porridge made of half-ground flour instead of oatmeal; and I shall most likely dine to-morrow on plantain fritters. Some other philosophers think that gentle exercise, as a branch of temperance, has also a share in illuminating the understanding. I am very fond of riding in an evening shower after a hot day; but I do not rest much upon this; my great dependence, for the expansion of my genius, is upon the porridge.'

'The cold, lifeless reasoning which is prematurely forced upon an unfortunate student at a college, is as different from the vigorous conception which is caught from mingling with general society, as an animated body from its shadow. It is distressing that we should persevere in the absurd practice of stifling the young ideas of boys of fourteen or fifteen with logic. A few pages of history give more insight into the human mind, and in a more agreeable manner, than all the metaphysical volumes that ever were published. The men who have made the greatest figure in public life, and have been most celebrated for their knowledge of mankind, probably never consulted any of these sages from Aristotle downwards.'

'We have for several years had a small detachment of two battalions with the Nizám. This is too trifling a force to give us any control over his measures; but it serves as a model for him to discipline his own army, and it compels us either to abandon him disgracefully in the hour of danger, as we did last year, or to follow him headlong into every war which he may rashly undertake. He is considered as more particularly our ally than either Tipú or the Maráthás; and it was, therefore, at the opening of his last unfortunate campaign, mentioned with exultation by our Resident, that there were in his camp above twenty battalions clothed and armed like English sepoys. I would rather have been told that there was not a firelock in his army. These very troops would have driven the Maráthás from the field, had they not been deserted by the great lords, with their bodies of horse and irregular foot, from cowardice, or more probably from treachery; and to reduce some of these turbulent, seditious chiefs, is now the principal employment of our detachment. Thus we are wisely endeavouring to render him as absolute a sovereign, and of course, from his greater resources of men and money, a more formidable enemy than Tipú.

'We ought to wish for the total subversion of both, even though we got no part of their dominions; but as it is not absolutely necessary that we should remain idle spectators, we might secure a share for ourselves; and were we in this overthrow of Tipú to get only his Malabar provinces, and Seringapatam and Bangalore, with the countries lying between them and our own boundaries, our power would be much more augmented by this part, than that of the Maráthás by all the rest. What are called the natural barriers of rivers and mountains, seldom check an enterprising enemy. The best barriers are advanced posts, from which it is easy to attack him, and to penetrate into his country, and both Bangalore and Seringapatam are excellent situations for this purpose. The balance of power in this country ought also to be formed on much the same principles—by making ourselves so strong that none of our neighbours will venture to disturb us. When we have accomplished this, their internal wars and revolutions ought to give us no concern. It is not impossible but that the Maráthá chiefs may settle all their differences without coming to hostilities; but if they should not, it is not easy to foresee what effect our preparations may have on Tipú.'

'The unity, regularity, and stability of our governments in India, since they have been placed under Bengal, and our great military force, give us such a superiority over the ever-changing, tottering governments of the native princes, that we might, by watching times and opportunities, and making a prudent and vigorous use of our resources, extend our dominion without much danger or expense, and at no very distant period, over a great part of the Peninsula. Our first care ought to be directed to the total subversion of Tipú. After becoming masters of Seringapatam and Bangalore, we should find no great difficulty afterwards in advancing to the Kistna, when favoured by wars or revolutions in the neighbouring states; and such occasions would seldom be wanting, for there is not a government among them that has consistency enough to deserve the name.'

'There are few of the obstacles here that present themselves to conquest in Europe. We have no ancient constitution or laws to overturn, for there is no law in India but the will of the sovereign; and we have no people to subdue, nor national pride or animosity to contend with, for there are no distinct nations in India, like French and Spaniards, Germans and Italians. The people are but one people; for, whoever be their rulers, they are still all Hindus; it is indifferent to them whether they are under Europeans, Musalmáns, or their own Rájás. They take no interest in political revolutions; and they consider defeat and victory as no concern of their own, but merely as the good or bad fortune of their masters; and they only prefer one to another, in proportion as he respects their religious prejudices, or spares taxation. It is absurd to say that we must never extend our dominions, though we see a state falling to pieces, and every surrounding one seizing a portion of its territory. We ought to have some preconcerted general scheme to follow on such occasions; for, if we have not, it is probable that we shall either let most of them slip altogether, or by acting in too great a hurry, not derive so much advantage from them as we might otherwise have done.'

CHAPTER V

THE THIRD MYSORE WAR

EVER since the treaty of Seringapatam, Tipú had been concerting measures to overthrow the English power in India; he had sent a mission to Constantinople, and another to Zemán Sháh, the ruler of Afghánistán, urging him to invade India; he also announced himself as the champion of the Muhammadan faith, whose mission it was to expel the English 'Kafirs,' as he called them, from the country, and with this object he was in treaty with both the Maráthás and the French. Thus Munro's forecast of the result of the policy of 1792 was verified.

At this juncture Lord Mornington was on his way out to assume the Governor-Generalship, and writing from the Cape, Feb. 28, 1798, to Mr. Dundas, he says:

'The balance of power in India no longer exists upon the same footing on which it was placed by the peace of Seringapatam. The question therefore must arise how it may be brought back again to that state in which you have directed me to maintain it. My present view of the subject is that the wisest course would be to strengthen the Maráthás and the Nizám, by entering into a defensive alliance with the former against Zemán Sháh, and by affording to the latter an addition of military strength and the means of extricating himself from the control of the French party at Haidarábád.'

Shortly after Lord Mornington's arrival at Calcutta not only were both these measures proceeded with, but having secured information of a proclamation by the French in Mauritius, calling on volunteers to take service under the 'Sultán of Mysore' against the English, he at once ordered preparations for an army to take the field against Tipú.

In February, 1799, a force of 20,000 men was collected at Vellore, and was supplemented by 13,000 furnished by the Nizám, under Col. Arthur Wellesley, afterwards Duke of Wellington, the whole army being under the command of General, afterwards Lord, Harris. On May 4 the war was brought to a close by the capture of Seringapatam and the death of Tipú, who was killed in the assault. Munro, who had attained his captaincy in 1796, was attached to a corps for collecting supplies for the main army and for demolishing small forts near Bangalore.

On the fall of Seringapatam Munro and Captain Malcolm[1] were appointed secretaries to the Commission to arrange for the future disposal of Mysore and other territories, and for the settlement of questions arising out of the late war. In a letter to his father, dated August, 1799, Munro describes this third Mysore war, gives a long estimate of the character of Tipú, with details of his life, and thus concludes by giving

[1] Afterwards Sir John Malcolm, Governor of Bombay, 1827-1830.

his opinion of the treaty which resulted from the labours of the Commission:—

'You will see in the papers how the partition treaty has been made. I believe that it has not met with general approbation here. Had I had anything to do in it, I certainly would have had no Rájá of Mysore, in the person of a child dragged forth from oblivion, to be placed on a throne on which his ancestors, for three generations, had not sat during more than half a century. I would have divided the country equally with the Nizám, and endeavoured to prevail on him to increase his subsidy, and take a greater body of our troops; but, whether he consented or not, I would still have thought myself bound by treaty to give him his fair half of the country. I would have given the Maráthás a few districts, provided they consented to fulfil their last treaty with him; but not otherwise. We have now made great strides in the south of India. Many think we have gone too far; but I am convinced that the course of events will still drive us on, and that we cannot stop till we get to the Kistna. I meant, when I began this letter, merely to have given you the history of my fever, in order to account for my apparent negligence in writing, and to let you know exactly how I was left. You might have had worse accounts of me from other quarters; but I have, as usual, run into a long gossiping story of Tipú and his family. But he is now at rest; and this is the last time I shall trouble you with him.'

While secretary to the Commission, Munro formed

a friendship with Col. Wellesley[1], which lasted through life. In some correspondence between them in the following year they argue for and against the extension of British rule in India. Col. Wellesley was opposed to it, considering the extension already greater than our means, and that we had added to the number of our enemies by depriving of employment those who had found it in the service of Tipú and the Nizám, either in managing the revenue, serving in the armies, or plundering the country. 'As for the wishes of the people,' he adds, 'I put them out of the question; they are the only philosophers about their governors that I ever met with—if indifference constitutes that character.' In reply to this Munro maintained that 'every inch of territory gained adds to our ability both of invading and defending.' There are three things, he said, that greatly facilitate our conquests in this country; *first*, the whole of India being not one nation, but parcelled out among a number of chiefs, and these parcels continually changing masters, makes a transfer to us regarded not as a conquest but merely as one administration turning out another; *secondly*, the want of hereditary nobility and country gentlemen, and of a respectable class of men who might be impelled by a sense of either honour or interest to oppose a revolution; and *thirdly*, our having a greater command than any of the native powers of money—a strong engine of revolution in all countries, but especially in India.

Wellesley's next letter gives an account of his

[1] They had previously met at Tópur in the Salem district.

victory[1] over Dhundia, or Dhundaji, a Maráthá adventurer, and he makes no further allusion to the discussion than to say, 'I fancy that you will have the pleasure of seeing some of your grand plans carried out.'

Not the least interesting association with historic Seringapatam is the fact that there in the summer of 1799 the future conqueror of Napoleon and the future Governor of Madras discussed the projects of the latter for the extension of British rule in India—'projects which Munro lived to see carried out far in excess of his early expectations, and which Wellesley only a few years later did much to further by his decisive victory over the Maráthás at Assaye.'

'It may be a question,' observes Sir Alexander Arbuthnot, 'whether, if Munro had lived in the days of Lord Dalhousie, he would have approved of the annexation policy of that ruler in all its details. It may be that he would have doubted the justice of suppressing native rule in Nágpur and the policy of annexing Oudh; but there can be no manner of doubt that the proposal to restore Mysore to native rule, after it had enjoyed for nearly fifty years the benefit of British administration—a proposal which, having been repeatedly negatived by the highest authorities, was eventually sanctioned in 1867—would have encountered from him an opposition not less strenuous than that which was offered to it by Lord Canning and his successor in the Governor-Generalship.'

[1] September 10, 1800—the first occasion on which the future duke held an independent command in the field.

CHAPTER VI

Kánara and its Settlement

Among the territories ceded by the partition treaty after the fall of Seringapatam was the District of Kánara, which stretches along the west coast, north of Malabar and west of Mysore. To the charge of this District Munro was appointed by the Governor-General, and here he remained from July, 1799 till October, 1800. It was with much reluctance that Munro took up this appointment. 'I have now turned my back upon the Báramahal and the Karnátik,' he says, 'with a deeper sensation of regret than I felt on leaving home; for at that time the vain prospect of imaginary happiness in new and distant regions occupied all my thoughts, but I see nothing where I am now going to compensate for what I have lost—a country and friends that have been endeared to me by a residence of twenty years. I feel also a great reluctance to renew the labours which I have so long undergone in the Báramahal. It leaves few intervals for amusement or for the studies I am fond of, and wears out both the body and the mind. Col. Read has sent in his resignation, and I had anticipated the pleasure of sitting down in the Báramahal, and enjoying a few years of rest after so many of drudgery, for that country is now surveyed and settled, and requires very little attention to keep it in order. It is a romantic country, and every tree and mountain has some charm which attaches me to them. . . .

'I must now make new friends, for there is not a man in Kánara whom I ever saw in my life. Nothing would have induced me to go there, had I not been pointed out for the business of settling that country. I had at one time declined having anything to do with it; and only two considerations brought me, after wavering for some days, to accept of it; the one, a sense of public duty, and the other, the chance which I might have of being enabled to return a year or two sooner to Europe than I could have done by remaining in the Bárámahal; but I can have no certainty of this, as my salary is not yet fixed.'

Munro's dislike to Kánara and the life he had to lead there increased with his experience of it, and he applied to Mr. Cockburn, of the Board of Revenue, for a transfer to Mysore, the Bárámahal, or the Karnátik, saying he would be happy 'to get away from it on any terms.' In reply to this letter Mr. Cockburn wrote: 'I regret your situation should be so extremely irksome; the more so, as any attempt to procure your removal would be considered *treason* to the State. Such is the estimation of your services, that no one is deemed equal to the performance of the difficult task you are engaged in; and though I can consider no reward adequate to the sacrifice you make, yet I trust you will be able to overcome your difficulties, and that Government will do you ample justice when you have brought the country into some degree of arrangement.'

Whether encouraged by these words or not, Munro continued to work on, and at the end of a twelvemonth wrote: 'Everything was so new and all in such disorder on my first arrival that the whole of the last year has been a continual struggle against time to get forward and bring up arrears; in this one year I have gone through more work than in almost all the seven I was in the Bárámahal.'

Throughout his residence in Kánara, Munro, who had attained the rank of Major in May, 1800, kept up a correspondence with Col. Wellesley, the latter communicating to him accounts of his campaign in the Maráthá country, and subsequently of that in the Deccan culminating in the battle of Assaye.

These letters are printed in Gleig's *Life*, and are still most interesting reading. In Sir Alexander Arbuthnot's *Memoir* will be found an extract from a minute[1] by Munro on the defences of the Malabar coast, with reference to the contingency of a French invasion, Napoleon being then in Egypt. This minute was one of several memoranda which Major Munro was called on to prepare for the information of the Governor-General; in it he observes:—'Supposing that any body of Europeans, from 5,000 to 10,000, were landed in Malabar, the only chance they would have of

[1] Then first printed from the original MS. in the British Museum.

maintaining possession of their ground would be by getting possession of some posts which might be capable of sustaining a long siege, and by being joined by the Náir Rájás and the other petty chiefs between Cochin and Sadáshivgarh. We ought therefore to have no forts of great strength on the coast of Malabar. Those which we already have, are sufficiently strong to guard against a surprise, and to resist any enemy who has no cannon, which is all that is necessary. Were the French to get possession of them, they could easily be driven out again by an army from Mysore; and as the Náirs, &c. would see that their footing was precarious, they would be afraid to join them. Were we, however, to make any place particularly strong, one of those unforeseen events which frequently happen in war, might throw it into the power of the enemy. After they were in it, it would be difficult to dislodge them, and they might in consequence be able to stir up the neighbouring petty princes of the country to insurrection.'

In Kánara Munro maintained his practice of keeping a journal for his sister; which, in spite of his heavy official work, and the discomforts of the climate and of his mode of life, is written in the same buoyancy of spirit and humorous vein that characterizes his previous home-letters. From it, however, there is space for only the following extracts:—

'I am now literally, what I never expected to be, so much engaged, that I have not leisure to write private letters. From daybreak till eleven or twelve at night,

I am never alone, except at meals, and these altogether do not take up an hour. I am pressed on one hand by the settlements of the revenue, and on the other by the investigation of murders, robberies, and all the evils which have arisen from a long course of profligate and tyrannical government. Living in a tent, there is no escaping for a few hours from the crowd; there is no locking oneself up on pretence of more important business, as a man might do in a house, particularly if it was an upstair one. I have no refuge but in going to bed, and that is generally so late, that the sleep I have is scarcely sufficient to refresh me. I am still, however, of Sancho's opinion, that if a governor is only well fed, he may govern any island, however large.

'I left Kárwár yesterday morning, where the Company formerly had a factory, but abandoned it above fifty years ago, in consequence of some exactions of the Rájá of Sonda, who then possessed this country. I crossed an arm of the river, or rather a creek, about half a mile broad, in a canoe, and proceeded on foot, for the road was too bad for riding, over a low range of hills, and then over some rice-fields, mostly waste, from the cultivators having been driven away by frequent wars, till I came again to the edge of the river. It was almost one thousand yards wide; and as the tide was going out, it was extremely rapid; and as there was a scarcity of canoes, as well as of inhabitants, I was obliged to wait patiently under a tree for two hours, till one was brought. I was, in the meantime, beset with a crowd of husbandmen, as I always am on my journeys, crying out, "We have no corn, no cattle, no money! How are we to pay our rents?" This is their constant cry, in whatever circumstances they may be; for, as the oppressive governments of India are constantly endeavouring to extort as much as possible from them, their only defence is to plead poverty at all times, and it is but too often with just cause they do so. They think that, if they are silent, their rents will be raised; and I shall therefore be pursued with their grievances for some months, till they find, from experience, that I do not look upon their being quiet as any reason for augmenting their rents. The party that attacked me, though natives of this part of the country, are Maráthás; they speak in as high a key as the inhabitants of the Gháts, which, as a deaf man, I admire, but not their dialect, which is as uncouth as the most provincial Yorkshire. Our conversation about hard times was interrupted by the arrival of a canoe, which enabled me to cross the river, and get away from them.

'After a walk of about two miles farther, I got to my halting-place, at a small village called Ibalgarh. Though I had only come six miles altogether, I had been above six hours on the road. As my tent was not up, I got into a small hot hovel of a pagoda to breakfast. I forget how many dishes of tea I drank; but I shall recollect this point to-morrow. When I was done, however, as my writing materials were not come up, as the place in which I was was very close and hot, and as I knew my tent and bullocks would not, on account of the rivers, be up before dark, I resolved to make an excursion, and look about me till sunset.

'There is hardly a spot in Kánara where one can walk with any satisfaction, for the country is the most broken and rugged perhaps in the world. The few narrow plains that are in it are under water at one season of the year; and during the dry weather, the numberless banks which divide them make it very disagreeable and fatiguing to walk over them. There is hardly such a thing as a piece of gently rising ground in the whole country. All the high grounds start up at once in the shape of so many inverted tea-cups; and they are rocky, covered with wood, and difficult of ascent, and so crowded together, that they leave very little room for valleys between. I ascended one of them, and stood on a large stone at the summit, till dark. The view before me was the river winding through a valley from a mile to two miles wide, once highly cultivated, but now mostly waste; the great range of mountains which separates Sonda from the low country, about twelve miles in front, many branches running from it like the teeth of a great saw, to the beach, and many detached masses running in every direction, and almost all covered with wood. On returning home, I found my tent arrived, and it was as usual filled with a multitude of people, who did not leave me till near midnight. I continued my journey at daybreak this morning, over cultivated fields for the first mile, and all the rest of the way, about ten miles more, through a tall and thick forest, up a valley towards the foot of the Ghâts. The prospect would have been grand from an eminence; but as it was, I saw nothing, except the heavens above me, and a few yards on each side through the trees. I liked the road, because it was carrying me away for a time from a country I am tired of. My halting-place was on the edge of a small mountain stream. There was not a clear spot enough for my tent, though a small one; but I was in no hurry about it, as there was plenty of shade under the bamboos and other trees to breakfast.

'Kánara does not produce such a breakfast as you have every day in Scotland without trouble; mine was very bad tea, for I had been disappointed in a supply from Bombay; some bread, as heavy as any pebble of equal size in the stream beside me, made about a week ago by a native Christian of the Angedivas, perhaps a descendant of Vasco da Gama, and as black as the fellow himself. It was however to me, who had seen no bread for three months, less insipid than rice, and with the addition of a little butter, of at least seven different colours, a very capital entertainment. You, who have fortunately never been in this country, may wonder why butter is so rare. It is because the cows are so small and so dry, that the milk of fifty of them will hardly make butter for one man. They are all black, and not much larger than sheep; and as they give so little milk, no man makes butter for sale. Every farmer puts what milk his cows yield into a pot or a bottle, and by shaking it for half an hour he gets as much butter as you may lift with the point of a knife; when, therefore, the serious task of raising a supply of butter for my breakfast comes under consideration, my servant, before he gets a sixpennyworth, is obliged to go round half a dozen of houses, and get a little at each. The whole together is not more than you eat every morning to your roll. When I had finished breakfast, and was sitting, as an Eastern poet would say, 'listening to the deep silence of the woods,' the little stream running past me put me in mind of Alander, and led me insensibly to Kelvin, and to the recollection of the companions with whom I had so often strayed along its banks, and thinking of you amongst the rest, I thought that none of them, now alive, would feel more interest than you in——.

'20th Jan. [1800].—I was interrupted yesterday by the arrival of my cutcherry people. I meant, I believe, to have said that, as no person would feel more interest than you in my solitary journey through Sonda, I determined, as soon as my writing-table should arrive, to begin, at least, an account of it to you, whether I should ever finish it or not. The wood was so thick that it was not till after some search that a spot could be found to pitch my tent upon; it was an open space of near a hundred yards square, which had in former times been cultivated, and had since been overgrown with high grass, which had a few hours before our arrival been set fire to by some travellers (who were breakfasting and washing themselves in the river), because they thought it might afford cover to tigers. It was still burning; but some of it, nearest the shade of the trees, being too wet with dew to catch fire, afforded a place for my tent. The people who accompanied me were so much alarmed about tigers, that as soon as it grew dark they kindled fires all round, and passed the night in shouting to one another. I never go to bed to lie awake, and was therefore in a few minutes deaf to their noise; but either it or the cold awoke me about two hours before daybreak: having no cover but a thin quilt, I was obliged to put on my clothes before I went to bed again, as the only way to keep me warm. The thermometer was at 47°, which you would not think cold in Scotland; but at this degree I have felt it sharper than I ever did in the hardest frost at home. It is probably owing to our being exposed to a heat above 90° during the day, that we are so sensible in India to the chill in the morning. I continued my journey this morning on foot, for the road was so steep and narrow that it was in most places impossible to ride.

'The forest was as thick as yesterday—nothing visible but the sky above. The trees were tall and straight, usually fifty or sixty feet to the branches; no thorns, and scarcely any brushwood of any kind. No flowers spring from the ground in the forests of India; the only flowers we meet with in them are large flowering shrubs, or the blossoms of trees. The ground is sometimes covered with long grass, but is more frequently bare and stony. Nothing grows under the shade of the bamboo, which is always a principal tree in the woods of this country.

'After travelling about two miles I got to the foot of the Ghát, where I met some of my people, who had lost their way yesterday, and had nothing to eat. I am fond of climbing hills; but I ascended the Ghát with much pleasure, because it was carrying me into a colder region, because I should be able to travel without being stopped, as in Kánara, every four or five miles by deep rivers, and because I should again, at Haliyál, bless my eyes with the sight of an open country, which I have not seen since I left Seringapatam. On getting near the top of the Ghát, the woods had been in many places felled, in order to cultivate the ground under them, and I by this means had an opportunity, from their open breaks, of seeing below me the country through which I had been travelling for two days. It was a grand and savage scene—mountain behind mountain, both mountains and valleys black with wood, and not an open spot, either cultivated or uncultivated, to be seen. I was now entering a country which had been long famous for the best pepper in India—an article which had been the grand object of most of the early voyages to the coast of Malabar; but there was not a single plant of it within many miles. On reaching the summit of the Ghát, and looking towards the interior of the country, I saw no plains, and scarcely anything that could be called a valley; but a heap of hills stripped of their ancient forests, and covered with trees, from one to twenty years' growth; except a few intervals where some fields of grain had recently been cut.

'Neither in Kánara nor Sonda does grain grow annually, except in such lands as can be floated with water. On all hills, therefore, and rising grounds, and even flats, where water is scarce, a crop of grain can only be obtained once in a great number of years—the time depends on the growth of the wood. When it is of a certain height it is cut down and set fire to; the field is then ploughed and sown. If the soil is good it yields another crop the following year, and it must then be left waste from eight to twenty years, till the wood is again fit for cutting. All the land within my view had undergone this operation; every field had a different shade, according to the age of the wood, and looked at first sight as if it was covered with grain of various kinds; but I knew to my sorrow that nineteen parts in twenty were wood. My halting-place was much pleasanter than yesterday, it was an open plain of about half a mile in length, surrounded with wood, but neither so high nor so thick as to hinder me from seeing the hills beyond it.

'My baggage being all behind in the pass, I sat down under a tree, and entered into conversation with half a dozen of the inhabitants, the owners of the fields where we were then sitting. They consisted of the accountant of a neighbouring village, and five farmers, two of whom were Maráthás; but the other three belonged to one of the castes of Indian husbandmen who never eat any kind of animal food, nor taste anything, not even water, in any house but their own: they wore beards as long as those of their goats, and they looked almost as simple and innocent. They pointed to a few straw huts at the end of the field, and told me it was the spot where their village had formerly stood. It had been burned and plundered, they said, about four years before, by Yenjí Naik, who had acted as a partisan in General Mathews's campaign, and had afterwards continued at the head of a band of freebooters till the fall of Tipú, when he relinquished the trade of a robber. They had forsaken their abodes during all that time, and were now come to know on what terms they might cultivate their lands. I told them they should be moderate, on account of what they had suffered.

'21st January.—I asked them some questions about the produce of their fields. One of the bearded sages replied that they yielded very little; that it was sometimes difficult to get a return from them equal to the seed they had sown. Had I asked the question of any other Indian farmer, five hundred miles distant, he would just have given me the same answer. It is not that they are addicted to lying, for they are simple, harmless, honest, and have as much truth in them as any men in the world; but it is because an oppressive and inquisitorial Government, always prying into their affairs in order to lay new burdens upon them, forces them to deny what they have, as the only means of saving their property. An excellent book might be written by a man of leisure, showing the wonderful influence that forms of government have in moulding the dispositions of mankind. This habit of concealment and evasive answers grows up with them from their infancy. I have often asked boys of eight or ten years old, whom I have seen perched on a little scaffold in a field, throwing stones from a sling to frighten the birds, how many bushels they expected when the corn was cut. The answer was always—"There is nothing in our house now to eat. The birds will eat all this, and we shall be starved."

'The farmers are, however, as far as their knowledge goes, communicative enough where their own interest is not concerned. I therefore turned the discourse to the produce of a neighbouring district. One of the old gentlemen, observing that I had looked very attentively at his cumbly, was alarmed lest I should think he possessed numerous flocks of sheep; and he therefore told me, with some eagerness, that there was not a single sheep in Sonda, and that his cumbly was the produce of the wool of Chitaldrúg. I was looking at his cumbly with very different thoughts from those of raising his rents. I had not seen one since I left Mysore: it is the only dress of the most numerous and most industrious classes of husbandmen. They throw it carelessly over their head or shoulders to defend them from the sun; they cover themselves with it when it rains, and they wrap themselves up in it when they go to sleep. The rich man is only distinguished from the poor man by having his of a finer quality. It was in this simple dress that I had for many years been accustomed to see the farmers and goatherds in the Bárámahal, and when I saw it again on the present occasion it was like meeting an old friend: it prepossessed me in favour of the owner; it brought to my remembrance the country I had left, and it filled me with melancholy, while I considered that I might never see either it or any of my former friends again. Our conference was broken up by the appearance of my writing-table. I had placed it under a deep shade, on the side of a clear stream, little larger than a burn, where, after breakfasting, I wrote you yesterday's journal. Such streams seem to abound in this country, for I am now writing on the bank of such another, but under a canopy of trees, like which Milton never saw anything in Vallombrosa; the aged banian shooting his fantastic roots across the rivulets, and stretching his lofty branches on every side; and the graceful bamboo rising between them, and waving in the wind. The fall of the leaf has begun for some time, and continues till the end of February. It was their falling on my head, and seeing the rivulet filled with them, that put me in mind of Vallombrosa.

'It was so cold last night that I had very little sleep. I rose and put on all my clothes, and went to bed again; but as I had no warm covering, it would not do, and I lay awake shivering most part of the night. At daybreak I found, to my astonishment, the thermometer at 34. I had never seen it in the Bárámahal below 47. I continued my journey as usual, a little before sunrise, through a forest with a few openings, except where the wood had been cut down for the kind of cultivation I mentioned to you yesterday, or where there were a few rice-fields, but none of them half a mile in extent. Through the openings I had glimpses of the low hills on all sides of me, some of them covered with wood, some entirely naked, and some half covered with wood and half with grain. I met with several droves of bullocks and buffaloes, belonging to Dhárwár, returning with salt from Goa. I saw a herd of bullocks feeding near the road, and I was glad to find they were the cattle of Sonda, for they resembled in size and colour those of Mysore. There is hardly a cow in Kánara that is not black; but above the Gháts black is uncommon, four-fifths of them are white, and the rest of different colours. Men are fond of systems, and before I came here I had convinced myself that the diminutive size and the dark colour of the cattle of Kánara were occasioned by scarcity of forage, and the deluge of rain which pours down upon them near six months in the year; but the rains are as heavy and constant here as in Kánara—it cannot therefore be by them that they have been dyed black. I am not grazier enough to know what influence poor feeding may have on the colour of cattle; but, if I recollect right, the small breed from the highlands of Scotland are called black cattle.

'There is no want of forage in Sonda, for, wherever the wood has been cleared away, the grass is four or five feet high. On coming to the place where I was to pitch my tent, I found that the head-farmer of the village, by way of accommodating me, had prepared an apartment of about twenty yards square and eight feet high, made of long grass and bamboos: it had been the work of a dozen of men for two days. He was much mortified that I would not go into it. I preferred the shade of trees during the day, and my tent at night. His son attended with a present of a fowl and a little milk. It is the custom in India, and was formerly in Europe, for men placed in the management of provinces to live upon the inhabitants during their journeys through the country; the expense thus incurred, and frequently a great deal more, is commonly in this country deducted from the amount of the public rent. I told the farmer that, as I meant to make him pay his full rent, I could not take his fowl and milk without paying him for them; and that I would not enter his pandal, because he had not paid the labourers who made it; but that *I* should pay them, and order my cutcherry people into it. It cost me a good deal of time and trouble to persuade him that I was in earnest, and really intended that he should not feed any of the public servants who were following me.

'22nd January.—I am now again seated at the side of a rivulet darkened with lofty trees. I have come about ten miles; but as I understand that Supa is only four miles farther, I mean to go on again the moment I see my tent come up: for I am not sure that it is on the right road, and were it to miss me, I might be obliged to spend the night under a tree, which is not pleasant in such cold weather, when there is no military enterprise in view by which I might comfort myself with the reflection of its being one of the hardships of war. I passed the greatest part of the night in endeavouring to keep myself warm, but with very little success; the covering I had was too scanty, and all my most skilful manœuvres to make it comfortable were therefore to no purpose. The thermometer at daybreak was at 36. It was 78 yesterday in the shade at three o'clock, which is the hottest time of the day: it will, I suppose, be about the same degree to-day. Such heat would be thought scorching at home, but here it is rather pleasant than otherwise. I enjoy the sun when his beams find an opening among the branches and fall upon me, and were it not for the glare of the paper I would not wish them away. Nothing can be more delightful than this climate at this season of the year. The sun is as welcome as he ever is in your cold northern regions; and though from 70 to 80 is the usual heat of the day, there is something so light, so cheerful, and refreshing in the breezes, which are continually playing, that it always feels cool. They are more healthy and sprightly than the gales which sported round Macbeth's castle, where the good King Duncan said 'the martins delighted to build.' My road to-day was an avenue of twenty or thirty yards broad through the forest. The trees were taller and thicker than I had yet seen them. The bending branches of the bamboo frequently met and formed a kind of Gothic arch. I passed many small rice-fields, and five or six rivulets.

'The most extensive prospect I had the whole way was over a flat of rice-fields, about a quarter of a mile wide and a mile long, bounded at the farther end by a group of conical hills covered with wood, beyond which I could not see. It was in woods like these that the knights and ladies of romance loved to roam; but the birds that inhabit them are not the musical choristers who, at the approach of Aurora, or when a beautiful damsel opened her dazzling eyes and shed a blaze of light over the world, were ever ready with their songs. They do certainly preserve the ancient custom here of hailing the appearance of Aurora; but it is with chirping and chattering, and every sort of noise but music. I must however except some species of the dove and jungle-cock; for though they cannot warble, the one has a plaintive and the other a wild note, that is extremely pleasing. The lark is the only musical bird I have met with in India. But notwithstanding the want of music and damsels, I love to rise before the sun and prick my steed through these woods and wilds under a serene sky, from which I am sure no shower will descend for many months.

'31st January.—I have been for these eight days past at Supa, a miserable mud fort, garrisoned by a company of sepoys. The village belonging to it contains about a dozen of huts, situated at the junction of two deep sluggish rivers. The jungle is close to it on every side, and the bamboos and forest trees with which, since the creation, the surrounding hills are covered, seem scarcely to have been disturbed. Every evening after sunset a thick vapour rose from the river and hid every object from view till two hours after sunrise. I was very glad this morning to leave such a dismal place. I had for my companion, every day at dinner, the officer who commanded. He was one of those insipid souls whose society makes solitude more tiresome. I was, to my great surprise, attacked one morning by a party of four officers from Goa, headed by Sir William Clarke. He was going as far as Haliyál to see the country. I told him he ought to begin where he proposed ending, for that all on this side of it was such a jungle that he never would see a hundred yards before him, and that all beyond it was an open country. He had put himself under the direction of an engineer officer as his guide, and had fixed on a spot some miles farther on for their encampment, so that he could only stay about an hour with me. He gave me the first account of the Duke of York's landing in Holland; but the overland packet, he said, brought nothing from Egypt.

'The country through which I came to-day was

a continuation of the same forest, through which I have now been riding about sixty miles. My ride to-day was about twelve miles; not a single hut, and only one cultivated field in all that distance. After the first four miles I got rid of the hilly, uneven country in which I had so long been; and the latter part of my journey was over a level country, still covered with wood, but the trees neither so tall, nor growing so close together, as those I had left behind. I could have walked, and even in many places rode, across the wood in different directions, which would have been impossible on any of the preceding days. I have halted under a large banian tree, in the middle of a circular open space about five or six hundred yards in diameter. One half of it is occupied by a natural tank covered with water-lilies. The rest is a field which was cultivated last year. It was just in such a forest as this that the characters in *As You Like It* used to ramble.

'What an idle life I have led since I came to India! In all that long course of years, which I look back to sometimes with joy, sometimes with grief, I have scarcely read five plays, and only one novel. I have dissipated my precious time in reading a little history, and a great deal of newspapers, and politics, and Persian. I am not sure that I have looked into Shakespeare since I left home; had I had a volume of him in my pocket, I might have read the *Midsummer Night's Dream* while I was sitting two hours under the banian tree, waiting for my writing-table and breakfast; but instead of this, I entered into high converse with a Maráthá boy who was tending a few cows. He told me that they gave each about a quart of milk a day; this is a great deal in India. Twenty cows would hardly give so much in Kánara. He told me also that the cows, and the field where we sat, belonged to a Siddee. I asked him what he meant by a Siddee. He said a Hubshee. This is the name by which the Abyssinians are distinguished in India. He told me that his master lived in a village in the wood, near a mile distant, which consisted of about twenty houses, all inhabited by Hubshees. I was almost tempted to suspect that the boy was an evil sprite, and that the Hubshees were magicians, who had sent him out with a flock of cows, who might be necromancers for anything that I knew, to waylay me, or decoy me to their den. But I soon recollected that I had read of Africans being in considerable numbers in this part of India. They are, no doubt, the descendants of the African slaves formerly imported in great numbers by the kings of Bíjapur and the other Muhammadan princes of the Deccan, to be employed in their armies, who were sometimes so powerful as to be able to usurp the government.

'15th March.—This letter ought, by this time, to have been half way to Europe; but I have had so much to do, and have had so many letters, public and private, on my hands for the last six weeks, that I never thought of you. I went in the evening, after talking with the cowherd, to see his master. He was a young boy, whose father had been hanged for robbery some years before. I saw his mother and several of his relations, male and female, not of such a shining black, but all of them with as much of the negro features, and as ugly as their ancestors were in Africa two centuries ago. I am now about seventy-five miles south of their village; but by traversing the country in different directions, I have come above twice that distance. I am encamped on the bank of a little river, called the Wurdee, and am within about two miles of the borders of Nuggur, usually called by us Biddanore. I have now seen the whole of the Sonda; and it is nothing but an unvaried continuation of the same forest, of which I have already said so much. Along the eastern frontier the country is plain, and appears from ancient revenue accounts to have been about two centuries ago well cultivated and inhabited; but it is now a thick forest, full of ruinous forts and villages mostly deserted. The western part of Sonda, towards the Ghâts, is an endless heap of woody hills without a single plain between them, that never have, nor probably ever will be cultivated, on account of their steepness It is among them, in the deepest glens shaded by the highest hills and thickest woods, that the pepper gardens are formed. The plant is everywhere to be met with in its wild state, but its produce is inconsiderable. It is from the cultivated plant that the markets of India and Europe are supplied. The cultivators are, with very few exceptions, a particular caste of Bráhmans, who pass the greatest part of their solitary lives in their gardens, scarcely ever more than two or three families together; their gardens are but specks in the midst of the pathless wilds with which they are surrounded. They are dark even in the sunniest days, and gloomy beyond description when they are wrapped in the storm of the monsoon.'

CHAPTER VII

The Ceded Districts

So successfully did Major Munro administer the affairs of Kánara that the Government was loth to transfer him elsewhere. By the end of the fifteen months which he served in that District he had reduced it to a state of good order; the bands of freebooters were put down, the ráyats, assured of justice in the collection of the taxes, and free from the fear of plunder, resumed their habits of industry, and good government was established throughout the province.

At length the opportunity arrived when the Government was able both to gratify Munro's wish for a transfer from Kánara and to reward his services by a more important trust. By a treaty with the Nizám the British Government undertook to protect his territories from invasion, and entered into a general alliance with him, in return for which a force, composed partly of British and partly of native regiments of the Madras army, was to be (and has ever since been) maintained at Haidarábád, and is known as the Haidarábád Subsidiary Force. To meet the cost of these troops the Nizám on his part agreed to make over to the Company the territory he had acquired by the treaties of 1792 and 1799, and thus were ceded to British rule the Districts of Bellary, Cuddapah, &c., still known as the Ceded Districts. For the Collectorship of these new Districts Munro applied, and to this he was appointed, and assumed charge of his duties in November, 1800. Lord Clive, in making the appointment, observed that the 'wishes of so excellent a fellow and collector ought to be cheerfully complied with.' 'Pray tell him,' he adds, 'my desire of detaining him on the Malabar coast has arisen from my opinion and experience of his superior management and usefulness; but that his arguments have convinced me that his labours in the Cis-Tumbudra and Kistna province will be more advantageous than his remaining in the steam of the Malabar coast, although I should have thought that favourable to a garden.'

When Major Munro assumed charge of his new duties in the Ceded Districts, it is computed that there were scattered through them, exclusive of the Nizám's troops, 30,000 armed peons, under the command of some eighty poligars, or petty chiefs, who subsisted by rapine; bands of robbers, too, wandered through the open country, plundering and putting to death travellers who refused to submit to their exactions. Such a state of things could not fail to inure the inhabitants to the use of arms; almost every village had its fort or was surrounded by walls, the remains of which may be seen to this day. 'The ten years of Mughal government in Cuddapah,' writes Munro in Feb. 1801, 'have been almost as destructive as so many years of war, and this last year a mutinous unpaid army was turned loose during the sowing season to collect their pay from the villages. They drove off and sold the cattle, extorted money by torture from every man who fell in their hands, and plundered the houses and shops of those who fled; by which means the usual cultivation has been greatly diminished [1].'

The first step towards the settlement of the Ceded Districts was to subdue the poligars; many of them were expelled or pensioned, and all required to disband their armed followers. This was mainly done by General Campbell, whose headquarters were at Bellary, while Munro, with four assistants (one of whom was Mr. William Thackeray, uncle of the novelist), attended to the civil administration of the country.

Writing to Read in Sept. 1802, he thus describes his work and life as an itinerant collector: 'I have all the drudgery, without any of the interesting investigations which employed so much of your time in the Báramahal. The detail of my own division, near ten lakhs of star pagodas, and the superintendence of others, leave me no leisure for speculations. The mere common business of Amildars' letters, complaints, &c., often occupy the whole of the day; besides, I am taken up an hour or two almost every other day in examining spies, and sending out parties of peons in quest of thieves

[1] Mr. R. Sewell, Collector of Bellary, has recently printed a valuable memorandum of Munro's dated March, 1802, giving the history of eighty poligars in the Ceded Districts, and stating how he had dealt with each of them.

and refugee poligars. I am also obliged to furnish grain for three regiments of cavalry, and the gun bullocks, and to transmit a diary every month to the Board, to show that I am not idle. My annual circuit is near a thousand miles, and the hours I spend on horseback are almost the only time I can call my own.'

It was Munro's custom to travel about without any military escort; his reasons for doing so are given in a letter in which he had to explain the circumstances of an affray in which Mr. Thackeray nearly lost his life. In quoting this letter, Gleig observes that it is 'a document of great public importance even now, furnishing very satisfactory proof that a civil functionary in India is safer when travelling unattended, than if he be followed by a weak military escort.' The condition of India has so changed that the question has not to be considered as regards districts under British rule, now as quiet as any agricultural county in England; but, with the Manipur disaster fresh in our minds, Munro's account of this incident, and his views as to a small guard attending an official in a turbulent country, are well worth perusal.

'Since writing to you yesterday, I have received yours of the 3rd [Dec. 1801], giving me the alarm about Thackeray. I heard of it the 27th of last month, and instantly wrote to the General to send a party, and I have offered a reward of one thousand rupees for the patel of Tornikul, by whose orders the murders were committed. Such outrages are frequent in the Ceded Districts, particularly in Gurramkonda; but I do not write upon them, because it would only be troubling the Board to no purpose; and you would have heard nothing of the late affair, had Thackeray not happened to be upon the spot. Why did I suffer him, you say, to be without a guard? Because I think he is much safer without one. I traversed Kánara in every direction unaccompanied by a single sepoy or military peon, at a time when it was in a much more distracted state than the Ceded Districts have ever been, without meeting, or even apprehending, any insult.

'I do the same here:—there is not a single man along with me, nor had I one last year when I met all the Gurramkonda poligars in congress, attended by their followers. I had deprived them of all their cowle, and they knew that I meant to reduce them to the level of patels, yet they never showed me the smallest disrespect. The natives of India, not excepting poligars, have, in general, a good deal of reverence for public authority. They suppose that collectors act only by orders from a superior power; and that, as they are not actuated by private motive, they ought not to become the objects of resentment. I therefore consider the subordinate collectors and myself as being perfectly safe without guards; and that by being without them, we get much sooner acquainted with the people. A Naik's or a Havildar's guard might be a protection in the Karnátik; but it would be none here in the midst of an armed nation. Nothing under a company could give security, and even its protection might not always be effectual, and would probably, in the present state of the country, tend rather to create than to prevent outrages. However this may be, such a guard for every collector cannot be spared from the military force now in the country.

'The murders in Adoni seem to have originated in private revenge. I directed Thackeray to add a certain sum to the last year's jumma, but to let the people know that it would not be finally settled till my arrival in the district. Under the Nizám's government many heads of villages had gained considerably by the general desolation of the country, because they got credit for a great deal more than their actual loss by diminution of cultivation. It was necessary to raise the rent of these villages to a fair level with that of others in similar circumstances. The people who brought forward the information required for this purpose are those who have been murdered. They were all natives of Adoni, and one of them was a gumasta in the cutcherry. The village of Tornikul, like most others in the country, is fortified. The patel refused to agree to the increase proposed. The serishtadar, knowing that there would be no difficulty in settling with the inhabitants, if he were removed for a few days, ordered him off to Adoni; but, instead of obeying, he shut the gates, manned the walls, and murdered, in the cutcherry, the three men who had given in statements of the produce. These unfortunate people, when they saw the pikemen approaching to despatch them, clung for safety about the serishtadar, which was the cause of his receiving some accidental wounds. Thackeray, who was encamped near the village, hastened to the gate, and on being refused admittance attempted to get over the wall. The men above threatened, and called out to him to desist, saying that they had taken revenge of their enemies, but had no intention of opposing the Sirkar; and he at length, very properly, withdrew to his tent. This is the account given me by a peon who attended him.

'Now, had he had the guard, about which you are so anxious, it would most likely have occasioned the murder of himself and of all his cutcherry; had it been in the inside, it would have been easily overpowered by one hundred and fifty peons; and had it been at Thackeray's tent, it would have followed him to scale the wall, and brought on an affray, which would have ended in the destruction of them all. Nothing is more dangerous than a small guard in a turbulent country. The sepoys themselves are apt to be insolent, and to engage in disputes. Cutcherry people are, in general, too ready to employ them in overawing the inhabitants, and have very seldom sufficient sense to judge how far it is safe to go; and a collector will never meet with any injury, unless he attempts to employ force, which he will hardly think of when he has no sepoys. I am therefore against making use of guards of regulars. Thackeray has always had above a hundred military peons in his division. I shall give him three hundred more; and he can select an escort from them, who will be sufficient for his protection, if he does not try to scale forts. The conduct of the people of Tornikul, after the atrocious murders in the cutcherry, was certainly, with regard to him at least, extremely moderate, and affords a strong proof that he is personally in no danger. On the 22nd November, two days after the affair at Tornikul, three potails and curnums were murdered by another patel of Adoni, for giving true statements to the Sirkar servants. By looking at the map, you will see that Thackeray's division, lying at nearly equal distances from Gooty and Bellary, is better covered by a military force than any other part of the Ceded Districts.'

Munro's first settlement for revenue purposes was a village one; each village was assessed at a certain valuation, and the cultivators were held responsible for that sum. His next settlement was a step towards a ráyatwárí one, but though it was made individually with the cultivators, the village headman was held responsible for defaulting or absconding ráyats; but before the cultivation of 1801-2 could commence, it was necessary to make advances for the purchase of seed, of implements, of husbandry, of bullocks, for the repair of old or digging new wells, and even for the subsistence of the ráyat till his grain was ready for cutting. In 1802 Munro commenced his new survey settlement, which lasted for five years. The whole of the cultivable area of the District was surveyed, a number given to each field, the name of the holder was registered, and the assessment fixed. 'It is astonishing how Munro was able, with such rapidity, to organize an establishment, and carry through a work which was not only new, but detrimental to the interests of the village headmen, whose false accounts and concealments of cultivation were thus brought to light. . . . It is, on the whole, wonderfully correct, and though it never underwent the revision which Munro intended to apply to it, it is even to this day a safe guide in most village disputes[1].'

While so fully occupied with administrative work, and constantly on the move, Munro was called on by the Board of Revenue to give them a particular account in a diary of the way in which he spent his time. 'I cannot see,' he writes, 'what purpose it would answer here, except to hinder me from looking after more important matters.' The multiplication of reports, returns, and references of all sorts is in the present day the bane of Indian officialdom; if such work is done by the head of the office it takes him away from 'more important matters,' and if, as is generally the case, it is left to a subordinate, it is calculated to cause needless friction by the work or diary of an official in a responsible post being reviewed by a clerk or even an under-secretary. Munro thus sums up his objections to unnecessary diaries and details: 'To explain to my assistants would take more time than to write it myself; and to write it myself is to leave part of my business undone, in order to write about the rest; for the day is scarcely long enough to get through what comes before me; and

[1] *Cuddapah District Manual*, by J. D. B. Gribble, pp. 117-122.

I am therefore obliged to relinquish a great deal of detail, into which I often wish to enter. My time has been spent so much in the same way during the last three years, that it is very easy to give an abstract of it. I have had no holidays since I left Seringapatam in 1799. I have had but two idle days; one that I rode over to see Sidout, and another that I went forty miles to see Cuppage at Nandidrúg. I feel the effect that a long perseverance in such a course must always produce. I have had no bad health, but am perpetually jaded, and get through business much slower than I should do with more relaxation.'

But Munro had not merely to deal with the poligars and the ráyats, the Board of Revenue and the Government of Madras, he had also to cope with the forces of nature, which periodically leave man and beast without a return for their labours in the field, or more relentlessly sweep them all away. In 1802–3 the land suffered from drought and famine, and in the following years from excessive rains. In a report to the Board, Munro calculated that 1,000 tanks and 800 channels had been breached in the Cuddapah District, and he estimated the cost of repairs at seven lakhs of rupees. Without waiting for the orders of Government, Munro ordered his subordinates to spend an almost unlimited amount, and the repairs were so speedily effected that, the following years being good seasons, he was able to report that 'the settlement was nearly as high as it need be, and it is not likely that for some years it can receive any material augmentation.

CHAPTER VIII

Wellesley's Campaign in the Deccan and Correspondence with Munro

The treaty of Bassein, concluded in 1802 with the Peshwá of Poona, took the other Maráthá chiefs by surprise, and Sindhia and the Bhonsla of Berár joined forces and menaced the Nizám's dominions. Two British armies were sent against them, one under General Lake and the other under Wellesley; the latter, after taking Ahmadnagar, routed Sindhia's forces in the battle of Assaye in September, 1803. During this campaign Munro supplied General Wellesley with basket-boats and boatmen, bullocks for transport, and rice for the troops, and was in constant communication with him. In one of his letters, dated Anantápur, Aug. 28, 1803, Munro suggested plans for dealing with the Maráthás, to which Wellesley replied, 'I have arranged the conquest of Ahmadnagar exactly as you have suggested,' and expressed his regret that he could not have him as a Collector of it.

The letter from Wellesley that follows describes his tactics at the battle of Assaye; it was written to Munro as 'a judge of a military operation, and as he was desirous of having him on his side,' and was in answer to one from Munro, from which the following is an extract:—

'I have seen several accounts of your late glorious victory over the combined armies of Sindhia and the Berár man, but none of them so full as to give me anything like a correct idea of it; I can, however, see dimly through the smoke of the Maráthá guns (for yours, it is said, were silenced) that a gallanter action has not been fought for many years in any part of the world. When not only the disparity of numbers, but also of real military force, is considered, it is beyond all comparison a more brilliant and arduous exploit than that of Aboukir. The detaching of Stevenson was so dangerous a measure, that I am almost tempted to think that you did it with a view of sharing the glory with the smallest possible numbers. The object of his movement was probably to turn the enemy's flank, or to cut them off from the Ajanta Pass; but these ends would have been attained with as much certainty and more security by keeping him with you. As a reserve, he would have supported your attack, secured it against any disaster, and when it succeeded, he would have been at hand to have followed the enemy vigorously [1].

'A native army once routed, if followed by a good

[1] 'The men of those days were stronger, bolder, more outspoken, not so mealy-mouthed as we are apt to be, not frightened at losing an appointment: or Bruce could not have bearded Duncan as he did on April 13, 1804, or Munro—he who to his credit had come out to India a man before the mast—would never have had the courage to write to Arthur Wellesley that he had sacrificed more of his men at Assaye than was at all necessary, and have his letter taken in good part.'—DOUGLAS's *Bombay*.

body of cavalry, never offers any effectual opposition. Had Stevenson been with you, it is likely that you would have destroyed the greatest part of the enemy's infantry; as to their cavalry, when cavalry are determined to run, it is not easy to do them much harm, unless you are strong enough to disperse your own in pursuit of them. Whether the detaching of Stevenson was right or wrong, the noble manner in which the battle was conducted makes up everything. Its consequences will not be confined to the Deccan: they will facilitate our operations in Hindustán, by discouraging the enemy and animating the Bengal army to rival your achievements. I had written thus far when I received your letter of the 1st of October, and along with it another account of your battle from Haidarábád. It has certainly, as you say, been a "most furious battle"; your loss is reported to be about two thousand killed and wounded. I hope you will not have occasion to purchase any more victories at so high a price.'

'Camp at Cherikain,
Nov. 1, 1803.'

'My Dear Munro,

'As you are a judge of a military operation, and as I am desirous of having your opinion on my side, I am about to give you an account of the battle of Assaye, in answer to your letter of the 19th October: in which I think I shall solve all the doubts which must naturally occur to any man who looks at that transaction without a sufficient knowledge of the facts. Before you will receive this, you will most probably have seen my public letter to the Governor-General regarding the action, a copy of which was sent to General Campbell. That letter will give you a general outline of the facts. Your principal objection to the action is, that I detached Colonel Stevenson.

'The fact is, I did not detach Colonel Stevenson. His was a separate corps, equally strong, if not stronger than mine. We were desirous to engage the enemy at the same time, and settled a plan accordingly for an attack on the morning of the 24th. We separated on the 22nd: he to march by the western, I by the eastern road, round the hills between Budnapore and Jalna; and I have to observe, that this separation was necessary—first, because both corps could not pass through the same defiles in one day; secondly, because it was to be apprehended, that if we left open one of the roads through those hills, the enemy might have passed to the southward while we were going to the northward, and then the action would have been delayed, or probably avoided altogether. Col. Stevenson and I were never more than twelve miles distant from each other; and when I moved forward to the action of the 23rd, we were not much more than eight miles. As usual, we depended for our intelligence of the enemy's position on the common harkaras of the country. Their horse were so numerous, that without an army their position could not be reconnoitred by an European officer; and even the harkaras in our own service, who were accustomed to examine and report on positions, cannot be employed here, as, being natives of the Karnátik, they are as well known as a European.

'The harkaras reported the enemy to be at Bokerdun. Their right was at Bokerdun, which was the principal place in their position, and gave the name to the district in which they were encamped; but their left, in which was their infantry, which I was to attack, was at Assaye, which was six or eight miles from Bokerdun.

'I directed my march so as to be within twelve or fourteen miles of their army at Bokerdun, as I thought, on the 23rd. But when I arrived at the ground of encampment, I found that I was not more than five or six miles from it. I was then informed that the cavalry had marched, and the infantry were about to follow, but was still on the ground; at all events it was necessary to ascertain these points; and I could not venture to reconnoitre without my whole force. But I believed the report to be true, and I determined to attack the infantry if it remained still upon the ground. I apprised Colonel Stevenson of this determination, and desired him to move forward. Upon marching on, I found not only their infantry, but their cavalry, encamped in a most formidable position, which, by-the-by, it would have been impossible for me to attack, if, when the infantry changed their front, they had taken care to occupy the only passage there was across the Kaitna.

'When I found their whole army, and contemplated

their position, of course I considered whether I should attack immediately, or should delay till the following morning. I determined upon the immediate attack, because I saw clearly that if I attempted to return to my camp at Naulniah, I should have been followed thither by the whole of the enemy's cavalry, and I might have suffered some loss: instead of attacking, I might have been attacked there in the morning; and, at all events, I should have found it very difficult to secure my baggage, as I did, in any place so near the enemy's camp, in which they should know it was: I therefore determined upon the attack immediately.

'It was certainly a most desperate one; but our guns were not silenced. Our bullocks, and the people who were employed to drive them, were shot, and they could not all be drawn on; but some were; and all continued to fire as long as the fire could be of any use.

'Desperate as the action was, our loss would not have exceeded one-half of its present amount, if it had not been for a mistake in the officer who led the picquets which were on the right of the first line.

'When the enemy changed their position, they threw their left to Assaye, in which village they had some infantry; and it was surrounded by cannon. As soon as I saw that, I directed the officer commanding the picquets to keep out of shot from that village; instead of that, he led directly upon it; the 79th, which were on the right of the first line, followed the picquets, and the great loss we sustained was in these two bodies. Another evil which resulted from this mistake was the necessity of introducing the cavalry into the cannonade and the action long before it was time, by which that corps lost many men, and its unity and efficiency, which I intended to bring forward in a close pursuit at the heel of the day. But it was necessary to bring forward the cavalry to save the remains of the 79th and the picquets, which would otherwise have been entirely destroyed. Another evil resulting from it was, that we had then no reserve left, and a parcel of straggling horse cut up our wounded; and straggling infantry, who had pretended to be dead, turned their guns upon our backs.

'After all, notwithstanding the attack upon Assaye by our right and the cavalry, no impression was made upon the corps collected there till I made a movement upon it with some troops taken from our left, after the enemy's right had been defeated; and it would have been as well to have left it alone entirely till that movement was made. However, I do not wish to cast any reflection upon the officer who led the picquets. I lament the consequences of his mistake; but I must acknowledge that it was not possible for a man to lead a body into a hotter fire than he did the picquets on that day against Assaye.

'After the action there was no pursuit, because our cavalry was not then in a state to pursue. It was near dark when the action was over; and we passed the night on the field of battle.

'Colonel Stevenson marched with part of his corps as soon as he heard that I was about to move forward, and he also moved upon Bokerdun. He did not receive my letter till evening. He got entangled in a nullah in the night, and arrived at Bokerdun, about eight miles from me to the westward, at eight in the morning of the 24th.

'The enemy passed the night of the 23rd at about twelve miles from the field of battle, twelve from the Ajanta Ghát, and eight from Bokerdun. As soon as they heard that Colonel Stevenson was advancing to the latter place, they set off, and never stopped till they had got down the Ghát, where they arrived in the course of the night of the 24th. After his difficulties of the night of the 23rd, Colonel Stevenson was in no state to follow them, and did not do so till the 26th. The reason for which he was detained till that day was, that I might have the benefit of the assistance of his surgeons to dress my wounded soldiers, many of whom, after all, were not dressed for nearly a week, for want of the necessary number of medical men. I had also a long and difficult negotiation with the Nizám's Sirdars, to induce them to admit my wounded into any of the Nizám's forts; and I could not allow them to depart until I had settled that point. Besides, I knew that the enemy had passed the Ghát, and that to pursue them a day sooner or a day later could make no difference. Since the battle, Stevenson has taken Barhampur and Asírgarh. I have defended the Nizám's territories. They first threatened them through the Caperbay Ghát, and I moved to the southward, to the neighbourhood of

Aurangábád. I then saw clearly that they intended to attempt the siege of Asírgarh, and I moved up to the northward, and descended the Ajanta Ghát, and stopped Sindhia. Stevenson took Asírgarh on the 21st. I heard the intelligence on the 24th, and that the Rájá of Berár had come to the south with an army. I ascended the Ghát on the 25th, and have marched a hundred and twenty miles since in eight days, by which I have saved all our convoys and the Nizám's territories. I have been near the Rájá of Berár two days, in the course of which he has marched five times; and I suspect that he is now off to his own country, finding that he can do nothing in this. If that is the case, I shall soon begin an offensive operation there.

'But these exertions, I fear, cannot last; and yet, if they are relaxed, such is the total absence of all government and means of defence in this country, that it must fall. It makes me sick to have anything to do with them; and it is impossible to describe their state. Pray exert yourself for Bistnapa Pandit, and believe me ever yours most sincerely, ARTHUR WELLESLEY.'

In reply to the foregoing, Munro wrote:—'Dear General, I have received your letter of the 1st instant, and have read with great pleasure and interest your clear and satisfactory account of the battle of Assaye. You say you wish to have my opinion on your side; if it can be of any use to you, you have it on your side, not only in that battle, but in the conduct of the campaign. The merit of this last is exclusively your own; the success of every battle must always be shared, in some degree, by the most skilful General with his troops. I must own I have always been averse to the practice of carrying on war with too many scattered armies, and also of fighting battles by the combined attacks of separate divisions. When several armies invade a country on separate sides, unless each of them is separately a match for the enemy's whole army, there is always a danger of their being defeated one after another; because, having a shorter distance to march, he may draw his force together, and march upon a particular army before it can be supported. When a great army is encamped in separate divisions, it must, of course, be attacked in separate columns. But Indian armies are usually crowded together on a spot, and will, I imagine, be more easily routed by a single attack, than by two or three separate attacks by the same force. I see perfectly the necessity of your advancing by one route, and Colonel Stevenson by another, in order to get clear of the defiles in one day; I know also that you could not have reconnoitred the enemy's position without carrying on your whole army; but I have still some doubts whether the immediate attack was, under all circumstances, the best measure you could have adopted.

'Your objections to delay are, that the enemy might have gone off and frustrated your design of bringing them to battle, or that you might have lost the advantage of attack, by their attacking you in the morning.

The considerations which would have made me hesitate are, that you could hardly expect to defeat the enemy with less than half the loss you actually suffered; that after breaking their infantry, your cavalry, even when entire, was not sufficiently strong to pursue any distance, without which you could not have done so much execution among them as to counterbalance your own loss; and lastly, that there was a possibility of your being repulsed; in which case, the great superiority of the enemy's cavalry, with some degree of spirit which they would have derived from success, might have rendered a retreat impracticable. Suppose that you had not advanced to the attack, but remained under arms, after reconnoitring at long-shot distance, I am convinced that the enemy would have decamped in the night, and as you could have instantly followed them, they would have been obliged to leave all or most of their guns behind. If they ventured to keep their position, which seems to me incredible, the result would still have been equally favourable; you might have attacked them in the course of the night; their artillery would have been of little use in the dark; it would have fallen into your hands, and their loss of men would very likely have been greater than yours. If they determined to attack you in the morning, as far as I can judge from the different reports that I have heard of the ground, I think it would have been the most desirable event that could have happened, for you would have had it in your power to attack them, either in the operation of passing the river, or after the whole had passed, but before they were completely formed. They must, however, have known that Stevenson was approaching, and that he might possibly join you in the morning, and this circumstance alone would, I have no doubt, have induced them to retreat in the night. Your mode of attack, though it might not have been the safest, was undoubtedly the most decided and heroic; it will have the effect of striking greater terror into the hostile armies than could have been done by any victory gained with the assistance of Colonel Stevenson's division, and of raising the national military character, already high in India, still higher.

'I hear that negotiations are going on at a great rate; Sindhia may possibly be sincere, but it is more likely that one view, at least, in opening them, is to encourage his army, and to deter his tributaries from insurrection. After fighting so hard, you are entitled to dictate your own terms of peace.

'You seem to be out of humour with the country in which you are, from its not being defensible. The difficulty of defence must, I imagine, proceed either from want of posts, or from the scarcity of all kind of supplies; the latter is most likely the case, and it can only be remedied by your changing the scene of action. The Nizám ought to be able to defend his own country, and if you could contrive to make him exert himself a little, you would be at liberty to carry the war into the Berár Rájá's country, which, from the long enjoyment of peace, ought to be able to furnish provisions. He would probably make a separate peace, and you might then draw from his country supplies for carrying on the war with Sindhia.'

By the treaty which followed this second Maráthá war, concluded near the end of 1803, Sindhia ceded all claim to the territory north of the Jumna, and the Bhonsla forfeited Orissa to the English, and Berár to the Nizám.

In a letter to Wellesley, dated Madanapalli, February 20, 1804, Munro writes: 'I read yesterday, for the first time, with great satisfaction, your treaty with Sindhia; your successes made me sanguine, but it exceeds greatly my expectations, and contains everything that could be wished; more territory can hardly be desirable until we have consolidated our power in what we possess. This cannot be effected without an augmentation of every description of troops. . . . The Indian armies in the different augmentations that have been made since the fall of Seringapatam, have received no proportionable increase of Europeans, and the European force is in consequence much below the proportion which it ought always to hold to the native battalions. Though we have but little reason to apprehend any danger from our native troops, yet it is not impossible that circumstances may induce them to listen to the instigations of enterprising leaders, and support them in mutiny and revolt. After seeing what has happened among our own soldiers and sailors in England, we cannot suppose that it is impossible to shake the fidelity of our sepoys. The best security against such an event would be an increase to our European force, which ought to be, I think, to our native in proportion of one to four, or at least one to five.'

Munro's suspicions as to the fidelity of the sepoys were soon verified. In the fort of Vellore, about eighty miles from Madras, the members of Tipú's family had been placed after his death; and here in July, 1806, the sepoys rose upon their European officers, killed thirteen of them, and over eighty of the detachment of the 69th regiment; but fortunately Colonel Gillespie arrived with a troop of dragoons from Arcot in time to rescue the survivors and prevent the mutiny from spreading. This outbreak was supposed to be a plot to restore the Musalmán rule in India, but it is more probable that it was due to new regulations prohibiting the sepoys from wearing caste marks, which, with changes prescribed in their dress and the mode of wearing their beards, were believed by them to be made with the object of making them Christians.

In Munro's correspondence there are the following letters relating to this affair. The first of these is from Lord William Bentinck, Governor of Madras, who was recalled in consequence of the mutiny; the second is Munro's reply; and the third, the best account we have of it, is a letter to his father dated September, 1806.

'[*Private and confidential.*]

'FORT ST. GEORGE, *Aug.* 2, 1806.

'MY DEAR SIR,

'We have every reason to believe, indeed undoubtedly to know, that the emissaries and adherents of the sons of Tipú Sultán have been most active below the Gháts, and it is said that the same intrigues have been carrying on above the Gháts. Great reliance is said to have been placed upon the Gurramkonda Poligars by the princes. I recommend you to use the utmost vigilance and precaution; and you are hereby authorized, upon any symptom or appearance of insurrection, to take such measures as you may deem necessary. Let me advise you not to place too much dependence on any of the native troops. It is impossible at this moment to say how far both native infantry and cavalry may stand by us in case of need. It has been ingeniously worked up into a question of religion. The minds of the soldiery have been inflamed to the highest state of discontent and disaffection, and upon this feeling has been built the reestablishment of the Musalmán government, under one of the sons of Tipú Sultán. It is hardly credible that such progress could have been made in so short a time, and without the knowledge of any of us. But, believe me, the conspiracy has extended beyond all belief, and has reached the most remote parts of our army; and the intrigue has appeared to have been everywhere most successfully carried on. The capture of Vellore, and other decided measures in contemplation, accompanied by extreme vigilance on all parts, will, I trust, still prevent a great explosion.

'I remain, my dear Sir, your obedient servant,

W. BENTINCK.'

Munro replied, from Anantápur, as follows:—'I have had the honour to receive your Lordship's letter of the 2nd [August]. On the first alarm of the conspiracy at Vellore, I despatched orders to watch the proceedings of the principal people of Gurramkonda, for I immediately suspected that the sons of Tipú Sultán were concerned, and I concluded that if they had extended their intrigues beyond Vellore, the most likely places for them to begin with were Chitaldrúg, Nandidrúg, Gurramkonda, and Seringapatam.

'Gurramkonda is perhaps the quarter in which they would find most adherents, not from anything that has recently happened, but from its cheapness having rendered it the residence of a great number of the disbanded troops of their father, and from the ancestors of Cummer ul Din Khán having been hereditary Killadars of Gurramkonda under the Mughal Empire, before their connexion with Haidar Alí, and acquired a certain degree of influence in the district which is hardly yet done away. The family of Cummer ul Din is the only one of any consequence attached by the ties of relationship to that of Tipú Sultán; and I do not think that it has sufficient weight to be at all dangerous without the limits of Gurramkonda.

'The Poligars, I am convinced, never will run any risk for the sake of Tipú's family. Some of them would be well pleased to join in disturbances of any kind, not with the view of supporting a new government, but of rendering themselves more independent. The most restless among them, the Ghuttim man, is fortunately in confinement; and I imagine that the others have had little or no correspondence with the princes. Had it been carried to any length, I should most likely have heard of it from some of the Poligars themselves.

'The restoration of the Sultán never could alone have been the motive for such a conspiracy. Such an event could have been desirable to none of the Hindus who form the bulk of the native troops, and to only a part of the Musalmáns. During the invasion of the Karnátik by Haidar, the native troops, though ten or twelve months in arrear, though exposed to privations of every kind, though tempted by offers of reward, and though they saw that many who had gone over to him were raised to distinguished situations, never mutinied or showed any signs even of discontent. Occasional mutinies have occurred since that period, but they were always partial, and had no other object than the removal of some particular grievance. The extensive range of the late conspiracy can only be accounted for by the General Orders having been converted into an attack upon religious ceremonies; and though the regulations had undoubtedly no such object, it must be confessed that the prohibition of the marks of caste was well calculated to enable artful leaders to inflame the minds of the ignorant—for there is nothing so absurd but that they will believe it when made a question of religion. However strange it may appear to Europeans, I know that the general opinion of the most intelligent natives in this part of the country is, that it was intended to make the sepoys Christians. The rapid progress of the conspiracy is not to be wondered at, for the circulation of the General Orders prepared the way by spreading discontent; and the rest was easily done by the means of the tapal, and of sending confidential emissaries on leave of absence. The capture of Vellore, and, still more, the rescinding of the offensive parts of the regulations, will, I have no doubt, prevent any further commotion—for the causes being removed, the discontent which has been excited will soon subside and be forgotten. The native troops, sensible of their own guilt, will naturally for some time be full of suspicion and alarm; but it is hardly credible that they will again commit any acts of violence.'

Writing to his father, Munro says:—'A very serious mutiny took place in June among the sepoys at Vellore, in which sixteen officers and about a hundred Europeans of the 69th regiment lost their lives. The fort was, during some hours, in the possession of the insurgents, but was very gallantly recovered by Colonel Gillespie, who happened very fortunately to be in the command of the cavalry at Arcot, and hastened to Vellore on the first alarm with the 23rd light dragoons and 7th regiment native cavalry. Some of his own letters, of which I enclose a copy, will give you a full account of the affair.

'A committee was appointed to investigate the causes of the insurrection. It has lately been dissolved; but I have not heard what report it has made. I have no doubt, however, that the discontent of the sepoys was originally occasioned by some ill-judged regulations about their dress; and that it broke out into open violence in consequence of being encouraged by the intrigues of Tipú, son of Moiz ul Din, then a prisoner in the place. The offensive article of the Regulations, which occasioned so much mischief, and which has since been rescinded, ran in the following words:

'"10th.—It is ordered by the Regulations, that a native soldier shall not mark his face to denote his caste, or wear earrings when dressed in his uniform. And it is further directed, that at all parades, and upon all duties, every soldier of the battalion shall be clean shaved on the chin. It is directed also, that uniformity, as far as is practicable, be preserved in regard to the quantity and shape of the hair upon the upper lip."

'This trifling regulation, and a turban, with something in its shape or decorations to which the sepoys are extremely averse, were thought to be so essential to the stability of our power in this country, that it was resolved to introduce them, at the hazard of throwing our native army into rebellion. One battalion had already at Vellore rejected the turban, and been marched to Madras, with handkerchiefs tied about their heads; but the projectors were not discouraged. They pushed on their grand design until they were suddenly stopped short by the dreadful massacre of the 10th of July. They were then filled with alarm: they imagined that there was nothing but disaffection and conspiracy in all quarters, and that there would be a general explosion throughout all our military stations. There was fortunately, however, no ground for such apprehensions; for almost every person but themselves was convinced that the sepoys, both from long habit and from interest, were attached to the service—that nothing but an attempt to force the disagreeable regulation upon them would tempt them to commit any outrage, and that whenever this design was abandoned, every danger of commotion would be at an end, and the sepoys would be as tractable and faithful as ever. Their discontent had nothing in it of treason or disaffection; it was of the same kind as that which would have been excited in any nation by a violent attack upon its prejudices.'

CHAPTER IX

MUNRO'S FIRST VISIT TO EUROPE

IN October, 1807, Lieut.-Col. Munro resigned his appointment as Principal Collector of the Ceded Districts, preparatory to going home on furlough. In reporting this to the Court of Directors, the Madras Government referred to his 'exertions in the advancement of the public service under circumstances of extreme difficulty, and with a degree of success unequalled in the records of this or probably of any other Government. . . . The general amelioration and improvement of the manners and habits of the Ceded Districts had kept pace with the increase of revenue; from disunited hordes of lawless plunderers and freebooters they are now stated to be as far advanced in civilization, submission to the laws, and obedience to the magistrates, as any of the subjects under this Government. The revenues are collected with facility, every one seems satisfied with his situation, and the regret of the people is universal on the departure of the Principal Collector.'

Col. Munro had for a couple of years previous to his departure been looking forward to a return home;

his remittances to his father and mother had placed them in comfort; he had bought a country house, Leven Lodge, for them; and he wished to see his parents again. But his long absence of twenty-seven years led him to anticipate few pleasures on his return to the old country, and what he was chiefly anxious about was what to do when he got home. 'I have no rank in the army,' he writes, 'and could not be employed upon an expedition to the continent, or any other quarter, and as I am a stranger to the generous natives of your isle I should be excluded from every other line as well as military, and should have nothing to do but to lie down in a field like the farmer's boy and look at the lark sailing through the clouds.' In another letter, addressed to his sister, he thus refers pathetically to the changes that time and distance had wrought:—

'You are now, I believe, for the first time, a letter or two in my debt; nothing from you has reached me of a later date than the 16th of May, 1804. This correspondence between India and Scotland, between persons who have not seen each other for near thirty years, and who may never meet again, is something like letters from the dead to the living. We are both so changed from what we were, that when I think of home, and take up one of your letters, I almost fancy myself listening to a being of another world. No moral or religious book, not even the Gospel itself, ever calls my attention so powerfully to the shortness of life, as does in some solitary hour the recollection of my friends, and of the long course of days and years that have passed away since I saw them. These ideas occur oftener in proportion as my stay in this country is prolonged; and as the period of my departure from it seems to approach, I look with pleasure to home; but I shall leave India with regret, for I am not satisfied with the subordinate line in which I have moved, and with my having been kept from holding any distinguished military command by the want of rank. I shall never, I fear, be able to sit down quietly to enjoy private life; and I shall most likely return to this country in quest of what I may never obtain.

'My resolution of going home has been strengthened by having this year discovered that my sight is not so good as it was. I find that when writing I must go to the door of my tent for the benefit of light when I wish to mend my pen. I endeavour to believe that this is entirely owing to my having lived so many years in tents under a burning sun. The sun has probably not shone in vain; but I suspect that Time has also had a share in whitening my hair and dimming my sight. His hand appears now before my eyes only thin and shadowy, like that of one of Ossian's ghosts, but it will grow thick and dark in a few years, and I must therefore return to my native land, and see my friends before it is too late.'

Colonel Munro arrived in England in April, 1808, but one chief object of his return to his native land was not to be gratified; his mother had died some months before he left India, and his father, who had all along followed with interest and pride the career of his distinguished son, had now become too infirm in mind and body to take an intelligent pleasure in his society. His own deafness, too, interfered much with his enjoying intercourse with his old acquaintances: 'some of them,' he says, 'stare at me, and think, no doubt, that I am come home because I am deranged.' His chief delight was in visiting the old spots, taking long walks, and 'rambling up and down the river.' 'I stood above an hour,' he writes, 'looking at the water rushing over, while the rain and withered leaves were descending thick about me, and while I recalled the days that are past. The wind whistling through the trees and the water tumbling over the dam had still the same sound as before; but the darkness of the day, and the little smart box perched upon the opposite bank, destroyed much of the illusion, and made me feel that former times were gone. I don't know how it is, but when I look back on early years I always associate sunshine with them.'

After spending some months in Edinburgh, where he again took up his favourite study of chemistry, Colonel Munro removed to London, and took an active interest in the politics and stirring events of the time. When the expedition to the Scheldt was fitted out, he accompanied Sir John Hope as a volunteer, and was present at the siege of Flushing.

While in London Munro was much consulted by the Court of Directors of the East India Company and the Government. The Charter by which the Company were invested with the government of India, renewed in 1793, was to expire in 1813, and the question of its continuance, especially as regards its trading privileges, was now being hotly discussed. Lord Grenville went so far as to oppose the continuance of the Company's territorial powers: he declared in a remarkable speech that 'twenty years was too long a period for farming out the commerce of half the globe and the government of sixty millions of people.' He held that the government of India ought to be vested in the Crown, that appointments to the civil service should be made by open competition and not by patronage, and that military cadetships should be conferred on sons of officers who had died in the discharge of their duties. Nearly fifty years, however, had to elapse before these reforms were carried out.

The mercantile interests, however, were too strong for a renewal of the trade monopoly, the abolition of which was merely a matter of time owing to the rapid extension of manufactures and to the fact that the war on the continent had closed many ports to British trade. The merchants of Liverpool and Glasgow successfully opposed the proposal of Government to limit the extension of the trade to vessels sailing from and to London, and the result was that, while the monopoly with China was continued to the Company for another twenty years, the trade with India was thrown open to the nation, with the restriction that no private vessel employed in it should be of larger dimensions than four hundred tons.

This whole question and other important matters connected with the internal administration of India—the system of land tenures, the judicial system, and the police—formed the subject of a searching enquiry before a Committee of the House of Commons. On all these subjects Colonel Munro gave evidence before the Committee, and, in the words of his biographer, 'among all those whose opinions were sought on that memorable occasion Colonel Munro made the deepest impression upon the House, by the comprehensiveness of his views, by the promptitude and intelligibility of his answers, and by the judgment and sound discretion which characterized every sentiment to which he gave utterance.'

In a long Minute on opening the trade of India to the outports of Great Britain, dated February 1, 1813, Munro gives an account of the various products of India, the exports and imports, observing that the imports from India might be increased and the price diminished by shorter voyages, and that every measure by which the demand can be enlarged and the supply facilitated of those commodities which do not interfere with our own manufactures promotes the national prosperity. He suggested that the culture of cotton in India might be improved by introducing American and other foreign cottons, and more attention paid to its clearing; raw silk, which had been imported from Bengal to the amount of about £600,000 per annum, might be increased to any extent, if protected by duties against the French and Italian; so also sugar, by a reduction of the existing duties. On the whole, he was opposed to throwing the trade open to the ports of Great Britain, and considered that the experiment should be first tried with London only. The following are the closing paragraphs of this very interesting Minute:—

'The Company are willing that the trade should be thrown open to the Port of London; but this, it is asserted, will not afford a wide enough range for the skill and enterprise of British merchants. But are these qualities monopolized by the outports? Have not the London merchants their full share, and have they not capital sufficient to carry on all the Indian trade which the most visionary theorist can look for? If freedom of trade is claimed on the ground of right, and not of expediency, every port in the kingdom ought to enjoy it; for they have all the same right abstractedly. But, unfortunately, it is necessary to withhold the benefit from them, because the warehouse system and customhouses are not yet sufficiently spread along our coasts; or, in other words, because a great increase of smuggling would unavoidably ensue.

'The East India Company are attacked from all quarters, as if they alone, in this kingdom, possessed exclusive privileges. But monopoly pervades all our institutions. All corporations are inimical to the natural rights of British subjects. The corn laws favour the landed interest, at the expense of the public.

The laws against the export of wool, and many others, are of the same nature; and likewise those by which West India commodities are protected and enhanced in price. It would be better for the community that the West India planter should be permitted to export his produce direct to all countries, and that the duties on East India sugar, &c., should be lowered.

'When the petitioners against the Company complain that half the globe is shut against their skill and enterprise, and that they are debarred from passing the Cape of Good Hope and Cape Horn, and rushing into the seas beyond them with their vessels deeply laden with British merchandise, they seem not to know that they may do so now—that all private traders may sail to the western coast of America; to the eastern coast of Africa, and to the Red Sea; and that India, China, and the intervening tract only are shut. Some advantage would undoubtedly accrue to the outports by the opening of the trade. But the question is, would this advantage compensate to the nation for the injury which the numerous establishments in the metropolis connected with India would sustain, and the risk of loss on the Company's sales, and of their trade by smuggling?

'The loss of the China trade would subvert the system by which India is governed; another equally good might possibly be found; but no wise statesman would overthrow that which experience has shown to be well adapted to its object, in the vain hope of instantly discovering another.

'It yet remains doubtful whether or not the trade can be greatly increased; and as it will not be denied that London has both capital and mercantile knowledge in abundance, to make the trial on the greatest scale, the danger to be apprehended from all sudden innovations ought to induce us to proceed with caution, and rest satisfied for the present with opening the trade to the Port of London. Let the experiment be made; and if it should hereafter appear that London is unable to embrace the increasing trade, the privilege may then, on better grounds, and with less danger, be extended to other places.

'If Government cannot clearly establish that no material increase of smuggling, and no loss on the Company's sales, and consequent derangement of their affairs, would ensue from allowing the outports to import direct from India, they should consider that they are risking great certain benefits for a small contingent advantage.'

In connexion with this subject a letter written by Munro when Governor of Madras to Mr. Finlay, a Glasgow friend, dated August 15, 1825, may be here quoted; not only as giving his opinions as a free-trader far in advance of his time, but as bearing on what is 'done against India' in the interest of Lancashire.

'I do not know that I have ever yet acknowledged the receipt of your letter about Dr. Anderson. I have never seen him, but I understand that he is a very good public servant; which, being our townsman, I consider as a matter of course. I hope that you are a friend to free trade for public servants, as well as for other articles; and that you do not think that men ought to have a monopoly of offices because they come from a particular town; or that we should call them China, when we know that they come from the Delft-house. I find, however, that there is no shaking off early prejudice, and becoming quite impartial, as a friend to free trade ought to be; I find that, notwithstanding my long exposure to other climates, I am still Glasgow ware; for, if I had not been so, I should not, when I saw your opinion quoted by Mr. Huskisson in support of his measures, have felt as much gratification as if I had had some share in the matter myself.

'I remember, when I was in Somerville and Gordon's house, about the time of the appearance of *The Wealth of Nations*, that the Glasgow merchants were as proud of the work as if they had written it themselves; and that some of them said it was no wonder that Adam Smith had written such a book, as he had had the advantage of their society, in which the same doctrines were circulated with the punch every day. It is surprising to think that we should only just now be beginning to act upon them; the delay is certainly not very creditable to our policy. Our best apology is, perhaps, the American and the French revolutionary wars, during the long course of which the nation was so harassed that there was no time for changing the old system. The nation was just beginning to recover from the American war, when the Revolution in France began; and had that event not taken place I have no doubt that Mr. Pitt would have done what we are now doing. I am not sure that you are not indebted to your old friend the East India Company for the measure not having been longer delayed. The attack upon their monopoly by the delegates in 1812-13 excited discussions, not only upon their privileges, but upon all privileges and restrictions, and the true principles of trade, which probably prepared the minds of men for acceding to the new system sooner than they would otherwise have done. Even now there seems to be too much solicitude about protecting duties; they may, for a limited time, be expedient, where capital cannot be easily withdrawn; but in all other cases why not abolish them at once? There is another point on which anxiety is shown, where I think there ought to be none—I mean that of other nations granting similar remissions on our trade. Why should we trouble ourselves about this? We ought surely not to be restrained from doing ourselves good, by taking their goods as cheap as we can get them, merely because they won't follow our example? If they will not make our goods cheaper, and take more of them, they will at least take what they did before; so that we suffer no loss on this, while we gain on the other side. I think it is better that we should have no engagements with foreign nations about reciprocal duties, and that it will be more convenient to leave them to their own discretion in fixing the rate, whether high or low.

'India is the country that has been worst used in the new arrangement. All her products ought undoubtedly to be imported freely into England upon paying the same duties, and no more, which English products pay in India. When I see what is done in Parliament against India, I think that I am reading about Edward III and the Flemings.

'I hope we shall talk over all this some day, in a ramble in the country, where the cows are still uncivilized enough to cock up their tails at strangers[1].'

[1] During Munro's visit home he was describing a military movement to Mr. Finlay in a field near Glasgow, in which some cattle were grazing; the animals, startled by his actions, rushed at them, and it was with difficulty they escaped over a wall.

CHAPTER X

PRESIDENT OF THE JUDICIAL COMMISSION

THE celebrated Fifth Report of the Committee of the House of Commons, published in 1813, drew public attention to the administration of justice and police in India. In both Bengal and Madras there were complaints of great delay in the disposal of civil suits and of the non-repression of crime. These defects were partly due to the fact that the judge of a District was also a magistrate, and, though a stationary officer, was invested with the superintendence of the police; and partly to the fact that the salaries of the native judges were too small to command either efficiency or integrity, and their number too limited to dispose of the litigation that naturally ensued on a settled government. Munro regarded the regulations passed by Lord Cornwallis in 1793 as too great a departure from native institutions, and advocated the revival of the 'pancháyat,' the transfer of the supervision of the police from the judge to the collector, and the appointment of village officials to deal with petty suits. These, with other proposals of his, were approved by the Court of Directors, who appointed a Special Commission to inquire into and reform the judicial system in the two Presidencies.

Of this Commission Colonel Munro was appointed President; and after a residence of six years at home he sailed for Madras again in June, 1814. He was now accompanied by a wife, having married in March Miss Jane Campbell, daughter of Mr. Richard Campbell, of Craigie House, Ayrshire, whose portrait, as Lady Munro, now adorns the drawing-room of Government House, Madras.

Munro landed at Madras on the 16th of September after a quick voyage of eighteen weeks; and in his first letter home he amusingly describes how his time was wasted in what he had never been accustomed to up-country—the system of calling and returning visits that still prevails in Madras. 'The first operation,' he says, 'is for the stranger to visit all married people, whether he knows them or not; bachelors usually call first on him—then his visits are returned; then his wife visits the ladies, and altogether there is such calling and gossiping, and driving all over the face of the country in an old hack-chaise, in the heat of the day, that I can hardly believe myself in the same place where I used to come and go quietly without a single formal visit. But all this is owing to a man's being married.'

The then Governor of Madras, Mr. Hugh Elliot[1], who had assumed charge on the same day as Munro

[1] Sir Thomas Munro was his immediate successor as Governor of Madras.

landed, seems to have been influenced by those around him to regard the changes proposed in the judicial despatch of the 29th of April, 1814, as unnecessary, for, to the civilian jealousy of a military collector or commissioner was added the fear that sweeping changes were intended by the Commission of which Munro was the head. Writing to Mr. Sulivan of the great delay the Commission was likely to encounter in the beginning, Munro says: 'Mr. Elliot received an impression very soon after his arrival, that everything was in the best possible state, that great improvements had been made since I left India, and that were I now to visit the districts, I would abandon all my former opinions, and acknowledge that the collector could not be entrusted with the magisterial and police duties without injury to the country.'

Six weeks later, when Munro had been nearly six months in the country, he wrote to Mr. Cumming, head of the Revenue and Judicial Department of the Board of Control, complaining that he was not now, as when he was in the Ceded Districts, acting without interference, and authorized to pursue whatever measures he thought best for the settlement of the country, but obliged before he could take a single step to wait for the concurrence of men who had always been averse to the proposed changes; and that the Government with its secretaries, the Sadr Adálat with its register, and every member of the Board of Revenue except one, were hostile to everything in the shape of the ráyatwárí system; and he advised that in their instructions the Board should not use such expressions as 'It is our wish,' or 'We propose;' that unless the words 'We direct,' 'We order,' are employed, the measures to which they relate will be regarded as optional. In a subsequent letter (March 14, 1815) he writes:—

'No orders have yet been issued for carrying into effect the instructions contained in the judicial despatch of the 29th of April, 1814; and the Commission consequently still remains at Madras.

'Mr. Elliot tells me that the resolutions of Government on the subject are printing for circulation, and that they correspond nearly with my view of it, except in not transferring the office of magistrate to the collector; but this is the most essential part of the whole, for without it the collector will be merely the head darogah of police under the zillah judge, and the new system will be completely inefficient. No time should therefore be lost in sending out, by the first conveyance, a short letter, stating the heads of alterations in the present system which are imperative, and not optional, with the Government here, and ordering them, not recommending, to be carried into immediate execution. . . .

'You will observe that in the two years 1812 and 1813 there was not a single appeal decided. I have looked at some of the appeal cases, and am sorry to say that much of the litigation is occasioned by the judges being in general very ignorant of the customs of the natives, and of the internal management of villages. This arises from very few of them having been ráyatwár collectors. I shall mention two cases which I read the other day.

'The first originated in the Zillah Court of Trichinopoli in 1808. It was a suit instituted by some Bráhmans to recover from the ráyats of a village 1800 rupees for their share of the crop, as Swámi Bhogum, or proprietor's right. The ráyats asserted that the contribution was not as proprietor's share, but voluntary to a pagoda. The curnum's accounts, which would probably have settled the matter, were refused by the judge in evidence, and the plaintiff cast. The Provincial Court reversed the sentence, and gave them a decree, not only for the money which they claimed, but for the land, which they did not claim. The Sadr Court ordered the whole proceedings of both courts to be annulled, leaving the parties to pay their respective costs, and begin *de novo* if they please.

'The second is a suit brought by a relation in the fifth or sixth degree of the Poligar of Woriorepoliam, to receive from the Poligar an allowance, in land or money, on account of his hereditary share of the pollam. He carries his cause in the Zillah and Provincial Court, and the sentence of the Sadr is not yet given; but I see on the back of the paper, in ——'s handwriting, "I think the decree of the Provincial Court is right." Now I am positive that they are all completely wrong.

'This cause, which has been going on for six years, would have been settled by a collector in half an hour. Indeed the plaintiff would not have ventured to bring his case before a collector; for among the military zamindárs, such as Woriorepoliam, Kalastri, Venkatagiri, &c., the nearest relatives, and far less the more distant, have no claim to the inheritance. The poligar usually gives to his brothers, &c., an allowance for their support, according to his own pleasure, not to any right. The plaintiff, I have no doubt, has been instigated by some vakil to make the demand; for, whatever happens, his fees are secure. The irregularity and negligence of some of the courts have been so glaring that the Sadr has been obliged to stimulate them by a circular letter. Stratton [1] wished to have established a more effectual check, by making them send reports showing the date of the institution of each suit, and of every document filed; but, though he could not carry this, and will often be obliged to satisfy himself with a protest, his exertions will make all the courts more active.

'The Commission, too, though it has not yet begun to act, does yet some good by its presence; for it is generally believed among the natives that it is authorized to inquire into all abuses, both in the judicial and revenue line; and this opinion has some influence in checking them. I have had ráyats with

[1] One of the judges of the Sadr Adálat, the then Chief Court of Appeal, selected by Colonel Munro to co-operate with him in the Commission. It was not without much demur that his wishes were acceded to.

me from almost every part of the country with complaints; but I have no direct authority to inquire into revenue abuses. I can only take them up where they are connected with the judicial system.'

At last, on the 30th of April, 1816, Munro was able to report to the Board of Control that 'the Commissioners' proposed Regulations may be considered as passed, as the Governor means to put their passing to the vote;' but he adds, 'they will be opposed in Council upon the necessity of waiting for all the heads of information required by the resolution of the 1st March, 1815, together with a report from the Commission of the potails and taliaries, fit or unfit, willing or unwilling, to execute the duties expected of them, and for the referring the regulations to Bengal for sanction previous to their being promulgated here. The information which was sought seemed to be required merely for the purpose of wasting time; no man who knew anything of potails or taliaries ever thought of asking them whether or not they liked their duty.'

The new Regulations, as eventually passed, are a monument not only of Munro's force of character in accomplishing his object against the most powerful opposition, but of his high administrative ability and statesmanlike views.

The most important of the changes effected by the new Regulations were the transfer of the superintendence of the police and the functions of magistrate of the district from the judge to the collector; the employment of hereditary village officials as police, and of the headmen of villages to hear petty suits; the extension of the power of native judges, the simplification of the rules of practice in the courts, and the legalizing a system of village and district pancháyats, or courts of arbitration—to which Munro attached much importance as being adapted to native habits and usages.

'Some of these measures have stood the test of the experience of half a century, and have been extended in principle if not in form throughout India [1]' On two points, however, the reforms of 1816 have not answered the expectations of their authors. The pancháyat system, being adapted to a primitive state of society, has not maintained its place by the side of the regular courts of justice, which speedily won the confidence of the natives; and the union of police and revenue functions in the native stipendiary officials, such as tahsildars, proved a mistake, resulting not only in a failure in the detection and repression of crime, but in a prolific source of oppression.

The 'Police' is now a separate force under European superintendents, and native or country-born inspectors; it is a half-military body, and performs many of the duties for which sepoys were formerly employed, and at present in only eight of the twenty-two Districts of the Madras Presidency is there a detachment of European or native troops.

[1] Sir A. J. Arbuthnot's *Memoir*, p. cxli.

CHAPTER XI

The Pindári and Maráthá Wars, 1817–1818

The work of the Judicial Commission had concluded before the end of the three years for which it was appointed. Colonel Munro had long coveted a command in the army, and the opportunity seemed now to have come. The great Maráthá chiefs had for some years lived as princes rather than as predatory leaders; but in their place, and secretly supported by Sindhia and Holkar, large bands of freebooters, known as Pindáris, with their headquarters in Málwá, made raids even into the provinces of Madras and Bombay. Preparations were being made by the Governor-General, the Marquess of Hastings, to repress these hordes, and Colonel Munro immediately offered his services. In January, 1817, he wrote to Lord Hastings suggesting that prompt action should be taken, observing that against native armies in general defensive measures are always ineffectual, but more especially against Pindáris; the great Maráthá armies have to halt occasionally for their baggage and supplies, but the Pindáris enter the country merely for plunder and not conquest;

'they can only be put down by seizing the districts in which they assemble, and either keeping them or placing them under a native government which can keep them under complete subjection.' He concluded by requesting that in the event of war he might be entrusted with the command of the subsidiary forces of Haidarábád and Nágpur and of such force as might be destined to act between the Godávari and the Narbadá. 'I am senior,' he wrote, 'to any of the officers now employed in that quarter; I have seen as much service as any officer in the Madras Army, having, with the exception of Lord Wellington's short campaign of 1803, been in every service with the army since June, 1780, when Haidar Alí invaded the Karnátik.' Other arrangements had apparently been already made for the military commands, but Munro was offered the Commissionership of the Southern Maráthá country, the Peshwá having ceded by the treaty of Poona in June, 1817, certain districts for the pay of the subsidiary force.

After taking up this appointment at Dhárwár, Munro wrote to the Governor-General stating that he could not but 'regret deeply to feel for the first time the army in advance shut against him,' and that his Lordship's plans did not admit of his being employed with the forces in the Deccan, but he was sensible that those plans ought not to give way to the views of individuals.

The remainder of this letter is a most important document, giving his views as to the evils which a subsidiary force entails upon the country in which it is established. 'It has,' he writes, 'a natural tendency to render the government of every country in which it exists, weak and oppressive; to extinguish all honourable spirit among the higher classes of society, and to degrade and impoverish the whole people. The usual remedy of a bad government in India is a quiet revolution in the palace, or a violent one by rebellion, or foreign conquest. But the presence of a British force cuts off every chance of remedy, by supporting the prince on the throne against every foreign and domestic enemy. It renders him indolent, by teaching him to trust to strangers for his security, and cruel and avaricious, by showing him that he has nothing to fear from the hatred of his subjects.'

Shortly after his assuming charge at Dhárwár, Munro was directed to reduce the Chief of Sandúr[1], which the Peshwá had required in accordance with the terms of the treaty with him. On Munro's arrival at Sandúr, in October, 1817, the chieftain Sheo Ráo, who had repeatedly declared that sooner than submit to the Peshwá he would bury himself in the ruins of his fort, came out and met Munro's detachment and, delivering up the keys, implored his protection.

[1] A little State within the Bellary District, containing the sanitarium of Rámandrúg. A recent Agent with the Sandúr Rájá, the late Mr. John Macartney, brother of Sir Halliday Macartney, will be long remembered for his excellent administration of the state and his exertions in the famine of 1876–78.

Munro, in reporting this incident to Government, stated that the Sandúr chief 'went through all the ceremony of surrendering his fort and abdicating the government of his little valley with a great deal of firmness and propriety, but next day, when he came to my tent with his brother and a number of his old servants and dependants to solicit some provision for them, he was so agitated and distressed that he was obliged to let his brother speak for him.' Munro made very liberal terms with him, and on his recommendation his little State was restored to Sheo Ráo after the conclusion of the war and the deposition of the Peshwá.

While Munro was engaged at Sandúr the Peshwá's forces were pushing south; but meantime a Brigadier's commission, with command of the division formed to reduce the Southern Maráthá country, was on its way to him. Though he had with him only five companies of sepoys, he determined to push forward and enter the enemy's country; and having already acquired the goodwill and confidence of the people of the newly-acquired districts, he resolved (to use his own words) 'to find the enemy employment in the defence of his own possessions,' and appointed military amildars to most of the districts in the enemy's possession, with orders to raise peons and to seize as much of their respective districts as practicable. While this was being done, General Munro took the important strongholds of Gadak, Damal, and Hubli, garrisoning each with the peons whom he had enlisted; he also issued proclamations offering protection to the cultivators, and announcing that the British Government would treat as enemies all who paid any tribute to the Peshwá or his agents. The people gladly obeyed these acceptable terms, not only refusing the demands of their own masters, but acting everywhere in aid of Munro's irregulars[1].

In a letter, addressed to Mr. Secretary Adam, dated February 17, 1818, Sir John Malcolm thus writes of Munro and his *modus operandi*:—

'I send you a copy of a public letter from *Tom Munro Sáhib*, written for the information of Sir Thomas Hislop. If this letter makes the same impression upon you that it did upon me, we shall all recede, as this extraordinary man comes forward. We use common vulgar means, and go on zealously and actively, and courageously enough; but how different is his part in the drama! Insulated in an enemy's country, with no military means whatever, (five disposable companies of sepoys were nothing,) he forms the plan of subduing the country, expelling the army by which it is occupied, and collecting the revenues that are due to the enemy, through the means of the inhabitants themselves, aided and supported by a few irregular infantry, whom he invites from the

[1] 'As General Munro advanced from the Karnatik he sent his irregulars to the right and left of his column of march, who occupied the villages, fought with spirit on several occasions, stormed fortified places, and took possession in the name of "Thomas Munro Bahádur."' Grant Duff's *History of the Maráthás*, ii. 484.

neighbouring provinces for that purpose. His plan, which is at once simple and great, is successful in a degree that a mind like his could alone have anticipated. The country comes into his hands by the most legitimate of all modes, the zealous and spirited efforts of the natives to place themselves under his rule, and to enjoy the benefits of a Government which, when administered by a man like him, is one of the best in the world. Munro, they say, has been aided in this great work by his local reputation,—but *that* adds to his title to praise. His popularity in the quarter where he is placed is the result of long experience of his talents and virtues, and rests exactly upon that basis of which an able and good man may be proud.

'I confess, after reading the enclosed, that I have a right to exult in the eagerness with which I pressed upon you the necessity of bringing forward this *master-workman*. You had only heard of him at a distance; I had seen him near. Lord Hastings, however, showed on this, as on every other occasion, that he had only one desire—how best to provide for every possible exigency of the public service.'

Though the Madras Government was not able to spare the troops intended for Munro, he continued his aggressive campaign, taking Badámi[1] and the much more important fortress of Belgáum, the only city still occupied by the Peshwá's troops, the capture of which

[1] On the Munro coat of arms there is a representation of an Indian hill-fort, with the word Badamy underneath.

supplied him with ordnance and stores, both greatly needed. The capitulation of Belgáum, still the most important military station in that part of India, took place in April, 1818; and Munro, having thus completed the conquest of the Peshwá's dominions south of the Kistna, was able to make a junction with General Pritzler's force. He then advanced on Sholápur, where was concentrated a force of over 11,000 picked troops—cavalry, infantry, and artillery—in the service of the Peshwá. After reconnoitring the fort, Munro decided on attempting an escalade of the walls of the pettah; the attack was made on the morning of May 10. The attacking party gained the parapet at a rush and were soon masters of the pettah; but meantime the enemy's artillery had attacked the reserve. Munro, taking advantage of the confusion caused by the bursting of a tumbril, led a charge, which the Peshwá's followers were unable to resist; they abandoned their guns and took shelter within their lines. The Maráthá chiefs now endeavoured to secure a retreat, and in the afternoon the whole army was in rapid march westward. Munro ordered the cavalry in pursuit, who completely routed the fugitive army, and within three days the garrison of the fort capitulated. The news of the capture of Sholápur and of the victory that preceded it showed the Peshwá that further resistance was useless, and contributed largely to bring about the negotiations which led to his surrender to Sir John Malcolm.

With the reduction of Sholápur the subjugation of

the Southern Maráthá country was complete, and General Munro, whose health was now much broken, sent in his resignation, and started in August, *viá* Bangalore, for Madras, in order to proceed home.

This chapter in Munro's history should not close without some extracts from the many interesting letters he wrote at this time. The following is from a letter to his wife, dated Damal, November 19, 1817:—

'There is nothing I enjoy so much as the sight and the sound of water gushing and murmuring among rocks and stones. I fancy I could look on the stream for ever—it never tires me. I never see a brawling rivulet in any part of the world, without thinking of the one I first saw in my earliest years, and wishing myself beside it again. There seems to be a kind of sympathy among them all. They have all the same sound, and in India and Scotland they resemble each other more than any other part of the landscape. . . .

'I have contrived to read the whole four volumes you sent me of the *Tales of my Landlord*. *The Black Dwarf* is an absurd thing with little interest, and some very disgusting characters. I like *Old Mortality* much; but certainly not so well as *Guy Mannering*. Cuddie has got a little of Sambo about him. His testifying mother is just such an auld wife as I have often seen in the West. Colonel Graham is drawn with great spirit; and I feel the more interested in him from knowing that he is the celebrated Lord Dundee. I admire Edith, but I should like her better if she were not so wonderfully wise—she talks too much like an Edinburgh Reviewer.'

Writing to Sir John Malcolm after his defeat of Holkar's army at Mehidpur, he says: 'Your battle while it lasted seems to have been as severe as that of Assaye; but I do not understand why you did not instantly follow up the victory, instead of halting four days to sing "Te Deum," and to write to your grandmothers and aunts how good and gracious Providence had been.'

From his camp near Belgáum he wrote to his sister (March 28, 1818): 'I cannot now write by candle-light; and it was after dark that all my private letters used to be written. But the great obstacle to my corresponding with you and my brother is the endless public-business writing, which comes upon me whether I will or not. Fortune, during the greatest part of my Indian life, has made a drudge of me; every labour which demands patience and temper, and to which no fame is attached, seems to have fallen to my share, both in civil and military affairs. I have plodded for years among details of which I am sick, merely because I knew it was necessary, and I now feel the effects of it in impaired sight, and a kind of lassitude at times as if I had been long without sleep.'

The following passages are from a letter to Sir John Malcolm, dated June 10, 1818:—

'You were present at the India Board office when Lord B—— told me that I should have ten thousand pagodas per annum, and all my expenses paid; and you may remember that you proposed that as the allowance differed only a few hundred pagodas from that of a Resident, it should be made the same. I never thought of taking a muchalka[1] from Lord B——, because I certainly never suspected that my expenses would, above two years ago, have been restricted to five hundred pagodas, a sum which hardly pays my servants and camp equipage; or that Mr. Elliot would have taken me by the neck and pushed me out of the appointment the very day on which the three years recommended by the Directors expired, though they authorized the term to be prolonged if deemed advisable. . . .

'With respect to myself, it is impossible that I can undertake the settlement in detail of any part of this country. I am as well with regard to general health as ever I was in my life; but my eyes have suffered so much, that I write with great difficulty at all times, and there are some days when I cannot write at all. Without sight nothing can be done in settling. It is a business that requires a man to write while he speaks, to have the pen constantly in his hand, to take notes of what is said by every person, to compare the information given by different men on the same subject, and to make an abstract from the whole. Since July last I have been obliged to change the number of my spectacles three times; and if you are a spectacle-man, you will understand what a rapid

[1] A written bond; see Yule's *Hobson-Jobson*.

decay of vision this implies. I cannot now do in two days what a few years ago I did in one, and I can do nothing with ease to myself. I cannot write without a painful sensation in my eyes of straining. The only chance of saving my sight is to quit business entirely for some months, and turn my eyes upon larger objects only, in order to give them relief. At the rate I am now going, in a few months more I shall not be able to tell a dockan from a breckan. Before this happens I must go home and paddle in the burn. This is a much nicer way of passing the evening of life, than going about the country here in my military boots and brigadier's enormous hat and feathers, frightening every cow and buffalo, shaking horribly its fearful nature, and making its tail stand on end. I shall willingly, now that all the great operations of war are over, resign this part of it to any one else. I am not like the Archbishop of Granada, for I feel that I am sadly fallen off in my homilies.'

The following is to Mr. Finlay, Lord Provost of Glasgow, dated Bangalore, September 11, 1818:—

'A great deal of fine cotton is grown in the provinces which have fallen into our hands. I was too much engaged in war and politics to have time to enter into inquiries regarding its fitness for the European market. The inhabitants have been so much impoverished by their late weak and rapacious Government, that it will be a long time before they can be good customers to Glasgow or Manchester. In those districts which I traversed myself, I fear that I left them no richer than I found them; for wherever I went, I appointed myself collector, and levied as much revenue as could be got, both to pay my own irregular troops and to rescue it from the grasp of the enemy.

'I shall not trouble you with military operations, as you will get the details in the newspapers. It is fortunate for India that the Peshwá commenced hostilities, and forced us to overthrow his power; for the Maráthá Government, from its foundation, has been one of devastation. It never relinquishes the predatory habits of its founder, and even when its empire was most extensive it was little better than a horde of imperial thieves. It was continually destroying all within its reach, and never repairing. The effect of such a system has been the diminution of the wealth and population of a great portion of the peninsula of India. The breaking down of the Maráthá Government, and the protection which the country will now receive, will gradually increase its resources, and I hope in time restore it to so much prosperity as to render it worthy the attention of our friends in Glasgow.

'Bailie Jarvie is a credit to our town, and I could almost swear that I have seen both him and his father, the deacon, afore him, in the Saltmarket; and I trust that, if I am spared, and get back there again, I shall see some of his worthy descendants walking in his steps. Had the Bailie been here, we could have shown him many greater thieves, but none so respectable as Rob Roy. The difference between the Maráthá and the Highland Rob is, that the one does from choice what the other did from necessity; for a Maráthá would rather get ten pounds by plunder than a hundred by an honest calling, whether in the Saltmarket or the Gallowgate.

'I am thinking, as the boys in Scotland say, I am thinking, Provost, that I am wasting my time very idly in this country, and that it would be, or at least would look wiser, to be living quietly and doucely at home. Were I now there, instead of running about the country with camps here, I might at this moment be both pleasantly and profitably employed in gathering black boyds with you among the braes near the Largs. There is no enjoyment in this country equal to it, and I heartily wish that I were once more fairly among the bushes with you, even at the risk of being "stickit by yon drove of wild knowte" that looked so sharply after us[1]. Had they found us asleep in the dyke, they would have made us repent breaking the Sabbath, although I thought there was no great harm in doing such a thing in your company.'

[1] See note on page 152.

CHAPTER XII

SECOND VISIT TO ENGLAND

IN January, 1819, General and Mrs. Munro sailed from Madras for England. At St. Helena the vessel stopped for some days, and Munro visited the spots associated with the presence of Napoleon. On May 30, when the vessel was in the latitude of the Azores, a son was born to him—the present Sir Thomas Munro. Towards the end of June, Munro and his family reached England, and proceeded at once to the homes of their friends in Scotland.

But his fame had preceded him; it was no longer confined to the Karnátik, the Bárámahal, or the Maráthá country. In a vote of thanks to the army, after the termination of the Maráthá War, Mr. Canning in the House of Commons thus alluded to the services of General Munro.

'At the southern extremity of this long line of operations, and in a part of the campaign carried on in a district far from public gaze, and without the opportunities of early especial notice, was employed a man whose name I should indeed have been sorry to have passed over in silence. I allude to Colonel

Thomas Munro, a gentleman of whose rare qualifications the late House of Commons had opportunities of judging at their bar, on the renewal of the East India Company's Charter, and than whom Europe never produced a more accomplished statesman, nor India, so fertile in heroes, a more skilful soldier. This gentleman, whose occupations for some years must have been rather of a civil and administrative than a military nature, was called early in the war to exercise abilities which, though dormant, had not rusted from disuse. He went into the field with not more than five or six hundred men, of whom a very small proportion were Europeans, and marched into the Maráthá territories, to take possession of the country which had been ceded to us by the treaty of Poona. The population which he subjugated by arms, he managed with such address, equity, and wisdom, that he established an empire over their hearts and feelings. Nine forts were surrendered to him, or taken by assault, on his way; and at the end of a silent and scarcely observed progress, he emerged from a territory heretofore hostile to the British interest, with an accession instead of a diminution of force, leaving everything secure and tranquil behind him. This result speaks more than could be told by any minute and extended commentary.'

Munro had already been thought of for an Indian Governorship; in August, 1818, the Governorship of Bombay being about to fall vacant, Mr. Canning submitted to the Court of Directors the names of

Sir John Malcolm, Mr. Mountstuart Elphinstone, and Col. Munro, observing that though it had been the 'practice of the Court to look for their Governors rather among persons of eminence in this country than among the servants of the Company, the extraordinary zeal and ability which have been displayed by so many of the Company's servants, civil and military, in the course of the late brilliant and complicated war, and the peculiar situation which the results of that war had placed the affairs of the Presidency at Bombay, appear to constitute a case for a deviation from the general practice.' 'The gentlemen,' he adds, 'whose names I have mentioned have been selected by me as conspicuous examples of desert in the various departments of your service, and on that scene of action which has been most immediately under our observation.'

All three of those named were destined to fill Indian Governorships. The Hon. Mountstuart Elphinstone was now selected for Bombay; he had been Resident at the Court of the Peshwá at Poona since 1811, and during the last Maráthá war had been brought into official communication with Munro, the former carrying on the campaign in the North Maráthá country and the latter in the South. Sir John Malcolm, Munro's old friend at Seringapatam, and like the other two also engaged in the last Maráthá war, succeeded Elphinstone as Governor of Bombay. Munro was in worthy company when named with these two, who formed two of 'perhaps the most illustrious trio of politicals whom the Indian services had produced.' His time soon came, for not many months after his arrival from India he was nominated to the Governorship of Madras in succession to Mr. Hugh Elliot, with whom he had had no too pleasant official intercourse when he was President of the Judicial Commission a few years previously.

Munro, who had before he left India been gazetted Companion of the Bath (Oct. 1818), was promoted to the rank of Major-General in August, 1819, and on his acceptance of the Governorship of Madras he was created a K.C.B. Before his departure for India Sir Thomas Munro was entertained at a banquet by the Court of Directors, at which his old friend the Duke of Wellington was present, as well as Lord Eldon and the rest of His Majesty's Ministers. In an eloquent speech Mr. Canning bore testimony to the high esteem in which the Governor-elect was held. In the course of it he said:

'We bewilder ourselves in this part of the world with opinions respecting the sources from which power is derived. Some suppose it to arise with the people themselves, while others entertain a different view; all, however, are agreed that it should be exercised *for* the people. If ever an appointment took place to which this might be ascribed as the distinguishing motive, it was that which we have now come together to celebrate; and I have no doubt that the meritorious officer who has been appointed to the Government of Madras will in the execution of his duty ever keep in view those measures which will best conduce to the happiness of twelve millions of people.'

Writing to a friend a day or two before he sailed for India, Sir Thomas said: 'I do not know that I shall derive so much enjoyment from the whole course of my government as from what passed that evening. It is worth while to be a Governor to be spoken of in such a manner by such a man.'

Sir Thomas and Lady Munro embarked for India in the middle of December, arrived at Bombay in May, where they were entertained for a fortnight by the Governor, Mr. Elphinstone, and thence proceeded by sea for Madras, where they landed on the 8th of June, 1820, and he was sworn in as Governor of Madras two days later.

In his diary for May 28, Mr. Elphinstone thus alludes to the visit of the Satrap of the Southern Presidency: 'Sir T. and Lady Munro went off. I am more than ever delighted with him; besides all his old sound sense and dignity, all his old good humour, simplicity and philanthropy, Sir Thomas now discovered an acquaintance with literature, a taste and relish for poetry, and an ardent and romantic turn of mind, which counteracted the effect of his age and sternness, and gave the highest possible finish to his character. I felt as much respect for him as for a father, and as much freedom as with a brother. He is certainly a man of great natural genius, matured by long toil in war and peace.'—Colebrooke's *Life of Mountstuart Elphinstone*, ii. 110.

CHAPTER XIII

GOVERNOR OF MADRAS, 1820–1827—ADMINISTRATIVE REFORMS

AT the time of Sir Thomas Munro's assumption of the Governorship of Madras there were many questions of special importance requiring settlement, and many reforms needed, not very palatable to the officials who represented the previous régime. How judiciously Munro himself acted may be inferred from the counsel he gave a few months after his arrival to Colonel Newall with reference to his appointment as Resident of Travancore. 'You will, I hope,' he writes, 'keep everything just as you find it, and let the public business go on as if no change had taken place. You will, like all new men coming to the head of an office, be assailed by thousands of complaints against the servants of your predecessor. You can hear them calmly and leisurely, and if you are satisfied that they have acted wrong you can remove them. But in all these matters too much caution cannot be used, and I hope you will write to me on the subject before you attempt any innovation. We have already, I think, made too many in this country.'

Writing in the following March to Mr. Canning he

says that, though he had not made any extension of the Regulations of 1816, he had 'never lost sight of the principles on which they are founded, namely, the relief of the people from novel and oppressive modes of judicial process; the improvement of our internal administration by employing Europeans and natives in those duties for which they are respectively best suited; and the strengthening of the attachment of the natives to our government by maintaining their ancient institutions and usages.'

On hearing that Canning had resigned his office of President of the Board of Control he wrote to him stating that he 'lamented it deeply both on public and private grounds,' and he then proceeds to give his views, novel at the time, on 'India for the Indians':—

'I always dread changes at the head of the India Board, for I fear some downright Englishman may at last get there, who will insist on making Anglo-Saxons of the Hindus. I believe there are men in England who think that this desirable change has been already effected in some degree; and that it would long since have been completed, had it not been opposed by the Company's servants. I have no faith in the modern doctrine of the rapid improvement of the Hindus, or of any other people. The character of the Hindus is probably much the same as when Vasco da Gama first visited India, and it is not likely that it will be much better a century hence.

'The strength of our government will, no doubt, in

that period, by preventing the wars so frequent in former times, increase the wealth and population of the country. We shall also, by the establishment of schools, extend among the Hindus the knowledge of their own literature, and of the language and literature of England. But all this will not improve their character; we shall make them more pliant and servile, more industrious, and perhaps more skilful in the arts,—and we shall have fewer banditti; but we shall not raise their moral character." Our present system of government, by excluding all natives from power, and trust, and emolument, is much more efficacious in depressing, than all our laws and school-books can do in elevating their character. We are working against our own designs, and we can expect to make no progress while we work with a feeble instrument to improve, and a powerful one to deteriorate. The improvement of the character of a people, and the keeping them, at the same time, in the lowest state of dependence on foreign rulers, to which they can be reduced by conquest, are matters quite incompatible with each other.

'There can be no hope of any great zeal for improvement, when the highest acquirements can lead to nothing beyond some petty office, and can confer neither wealth nor honour. While the prospects of the natives are so bounded, every project for bettering their characters must fail; and no such projects can have the smallest chance of success, unless some of those objects are placed within their reach for the sake of which men are urged to exertion in other countries. This work of improvement, in whatever way it may be attempted, must be very slow, but it will be in proportion to the degree of confidence which we repose in them, and to the share which we give them in the administration of public affairs. All that we can give them, without endangering our own ascendancy, should be given. All real military power must be kept in our own hands; but they might, with advantage hereafter, be made eligible to every civil office under that of a member of the Government. The change should be gradual, because they are not yet fit to discharge properly the duties of a high civil employment, according to our rules and ideas; but the sphere of their employment should be extended in proportion as we find that they become capable of filling properly higher situations.

'We shall never have much accurate knowledge of the resources of the country, or of the causes by which they are raised or depressed; we shall always assess it very unequally, and often too high, until we learn to treat the higher classes of natives as gentlemen, and to make them assist us accordingly in doing what is done by the House of Commons in England, in estimating and apportioning the amount of taxation.'

Among the matters that the Governor had to deal with were more than one to which residents in Madras in the last quarter of a century could find a parallel. In 1822 some trouble was caused by the efforts made by a sub-collector in Bellary to convert the natives to Christianity; and from Sir Thomas Munro's long and able minute on the subject, the following extracts are worth quoting:—

'Everything in the sub-collector's report is highly commendable, excepting those passages in which he speaks of the character of the natives, and of his having distributed books among them. He evinces strong prejudice against them, and deplores the ignorance of the ráyats, and their uncouth speech, which he observes must for ever prevent direct communication between them and the European authorities. He speaks as if these defects were peculiar to India, and as if all the farmers and labourers of England were well educated and spoke a pure dialect. . . .

'Mr. ——, in fact, did all that a missionary could have done; he employed his own and the district cutcherries in the work; and he himself both distributed and explained. If he had been a missionary, what more could he have done? He could not have done so much. He could not have assembled the inhabitants, or employed the cutcherries in distributing moral and religious tracts. No person could have done this but a civil servant, and in Harpanahalli and Bellary none could have done it but him; yet he cannot in this discover official interference. . . .

'He employs his official authority for missionary purposes; and when he is told by his superior that he is wrong, he justifies his acts by quotations from Scripture, and by election, a doctrine which has occasioned so much controversy; and he leaves it to be inferred that Government must either adopt his views or act contrary to divine authority. A person who can, as a sub-collector and magistrate, bring forward such matters for discussion, and seriously desire that they may be placed on record and examined by Government, is not in a frame of mind to be restrained within the proper limits of his duty by any official rules. . . .

'In every country, but especially in this, where the rulers are so few, and of a different race from the people, it is the most dangerous of all things to tamper with religious feelings; they may be apparently dormant, and when we are in unsuspecting security they may burst forth in the most tremendous manner, as at Vellore; they may be set in motion by the slightest casual incident, and do more mischief in one year than all the labours of missionary collectors would repair in a hundred. Should they produce only a partial disturbance, which is quickly put down, even in this case the evil would be lasting; distrust would be raised between the people and the Government, which would never entirely subside, and the district in which it happened would never be so safe as before. The agency of collectors and magistrates, as religious instructors, can effect no possible good. It may for a moment raise the hopes of a few sanguine men; but it will end in disturbance and failure, and, instead of forwarding, will greatly retard, every chance of ultimate success. . . .

'The best way for a collector to instruct the natives is to set them an example in his own conduct; to try to settle their disputes with each other, and to prevent their going to law; to bear patiently all their complaints against himself and his servants, and bad seasons, and to afford them all the relief in his power; and, if he can do nothing more, to give them at least good words.

'Whatever change it may be desirable to produce upon the characters of the natives may be effected by much safer and surer means than official interference with their religion. Regular missionaries are sent out by the Honourable the Court of Directors, and by different European Governments. These men visit every part of the country, and pursue their labours without the smallest hindrance; and, as they have no power, they are well received everywhere. In order to dispose the natives to receive our instruction and to adopt our opinions, we must first gain their attachment and confidence, and this can only be accomplished by a pure administration of justice, by moderate assessment, respect for their customs, and general good government.'

In the end of May, just before Munro's arrival in Madras, a riot, in which several lives were lost, took place in Masulipatam, between different castes, arising out of a dispute about ceremonies. In his Minute as Governor, dated July 3, 1820, he remarks as follows on the action of the collector whose 'well-known zeal had led him to adopt measures for the prevention of such disturbances, which if sanctioned would rather augment than mitigate the evil:—

'The collector's proposition is that all differences respecting procession and other ceremonies should be decided by the courts of law, and that, in the meantime, he should support the party whose claim seems consistent with natural right. He observes that the beating of tom-toms, riding in a palankeen, and erecting a pandál, are privileges which injure nobody, and naturally belong to every person who can afford to pay for them. This is very true; but it is also true that things equally harmless in themselves have in all ages and in all nations, and in our own as well as in others, frequently excited the most obstinate and sanguinary contests. The alteration of a mere form or symbol of no importance has as often produced these effects as an attack on the fundamental principles of the national faith. It would therefore be extremely imprudent to use the authority of Government in supporting the performance of ceremonies which we know are likely to be opposed by a large body of the natives. On all such occasions it would be most advisable that the officers of Government should take no part, but entirely confine themselves to the preservation of the public peace, which will, in almost every case, be more likely to be secured by discouraging, rather than promoting, disputed claims to the right of using palankeens, flags, and other marks of distinction during the celebration of certain ceremonies.

'The magistrate seems to think that, because a decision of the Zillah Court put a stop to the opposition given to the caste of Banians, in having the Vaduklam rites performed in their houses in the language of the Vedas, it would have the same efficacy in stopping the opposition to marriage processions; but the cases are entirely different. The Banians have the sanction of the shástras for the use of the Vaduklam rites in their families; the ceremony is private, and the opposition is only by a few Bráhmans. But in the case of the marriage procession, there is no sanction of the shástras; the ceremony is public and lasts for days together, and the opposition is by the whole of the right-hand against the whole of the left-hand castes, and brings every Hindu into the conflict.

'The result of the magistrate's experiment ought to make us avoid the repetition of it. We find from his own statement that the mischief was occasioned by his wish to restore to the caste of goldsmiths the right of riding in a palankeen, which he considered to belong to every man who chose to pay for it. He annulled a former order against it, in consequence of the complaint of the Zillah Court, that he was hindered by it from performing his son's marriage in a manner suitable to his rank; and as he did not apprehend any disturbance, he left Masulipatam before the ceremony took place. The assistant magistrate, however, two days before its commencement, received information that opposition was intended. He did whatever could be done to preserve the peace of the town, but to no purpose. He issued a proclamation, stationed the police in the streets to prevent riot, reinforced them with the revenue peons, and desired the officer commanding the troops to keep them in readiness within their lines. But in spite of all these precautions a serious affray, as might have been expected, occurs, in which property is plundered and lives are lost; and all this array of civil and military power, and all this tumult, arises solely from its being thought necessary that a writer of the court should have a palankeen at the celebration of a marriage. Had the writer not looked for the support of the magistrate, he would undoubtedly not have ventured to go in procession, and no disturbance would have happened.

'The magistrate states that this very writer had gone about for many years in a palankeen without hindrance. But this is not the point in dispute: it is not his using a palankeen on his ordinary business, but his going in procession. It is this which constitutes the triumph of one party and the defeat of the other, and which, whilst such opinions are entertained by the natives, will always produce affrays. The magistrate supposes that the opposition was not justified by the custom of the country, because it was notorious that in many places of the same district the goldsmith caste went in procession in palankeens. This is very likely; but it does not affect the question, which relates solely to what is the custom of the town of Masulipatam, not to what that of other places is. . . .

'It would be desirable that the customs of the castes, connected with their public ceremonies, should be the same everywhere, and that differences respecting them should be settled by decisions of the courts; but as this is impossible while these prejudices remain, we ought in the meantime to follow the course most likely to prevent disorder and outrage. The conflicts of the castes are usually most serious and most frequent when one party or the other expects the support of the officers of Government. They are usually occasioned by supporting some innovation respecting ceremonies, but rarely by punishing it. The magistrate ought, therefore, to give no aid whatever to any persons desirous of celebrating marriages or other festivals, or public ceremonies in any way not usual in the place, but rather to discountenance innovation. He ought, in all disputes between the castes, to take no part beyond what may be necessary in order to preserve the peace; and he ought to punish the rioters on both sides, in cases of affray, for breach of the peace, and on the whole to conduct himself in such a manner as to make it evident to the people that he favours the pretensions of neither side, but looks only to the maintenance of the peace.

'I recommend that instructions in conformity to these suggestions be sent to the magistrates for their guidance.'

It would be impossible to give in this volume more than an idea of the variety of subjects and the importance of the topics in the Minutes issued by

Munro. In the valuable collection of his Minutes and other official writings selected and edited by Sir A. J. Arbuthnot, there are over ninety papers under the heads of Revenue, Judicial, Political, Military, and Miscellaneous. Among them are Minutes on the settlement of Salem and of Kánara, the principle of the ráyatwárí system, on the revenue survey, on the state of the country and the condition of the people, on trial by Pancháyát, on the administration of justice, on the interfering with the succession of native princes, on the maladministration of Mysore, on recruiting the army by drafts from Europe, on relieving entire regiments, on reductions in the Madras army, on procuring military stores from England or manufacturing them in India, on the war in Burma, on the course to be taken by Government in dealing with a scarcity of grain, on import duties, on the Eurasian population, on the proper mode of dealing with charges against native officials, on pecuniary transactions between a European District officer and a zamindár, on the danger of a free press in India, on the employment of natives in the public service, and on the education of the natives of India.

On few reforms did Munro more frequently insist than the necessity of more largely utilizing native agency, and he strongly pointed out the impolicy of excluding the natives of India from all situations of trust. A passage on this subject has been quoted from his letter to Mr. Canning, and three years later in an important Minute on the state of the country and the condition of the people he once more argues the cause of the admission of the natives of the country to positions of trust and emolument. 'With what grace,' he asks, 'can we talk of paternal government if we exclude the natives from every important office, and say, as we did till very lately, that in a country containing fifteen millions of inhabitants no man but a European shall be entrusted with as much authority as to order the punishment of a single stroke of a rattan? . . . Let Britain be subjugated by a foreign power to-morrow, let the people be excluded from all share in the government, from public honours, from every office of high trust and emolument, and let them in every situation be considered as unworthy of trust, and all their knowledge and all their literature, sacred and profane, would not save them from becoming in another generation or two, a low-minded, deceitful, and dishonest race.'

Writing to Munro, Oct. 27, 1822, the Governor of Bombay, Mr. Elphinstone, says:—

'I hear you have instituted something like a Native Board of Revenue at Madras, and I should be much obliged if you would inform me of the nature of the plan. It seems to be one great advantage of the arrangement that it opens a door to the employment of natives in high and efficient situations. I should be happy to know if you think the plan can be extended to the judicial or any other line. Besides the necessity for having good native advisers in governing natives, it is necessary that we should pave the way for the introduction of the natives to some share in the government of their own country. It may be half a century before we are obliged to do so; but the system of government and of education which we have already established must some time or other work such a change on the people of this country that it will be impossible to confine them to subordinate employments; and if we have not previously opened vents for their ambition and ability we may expect an explosion which will overturn our government.

'I should be much obliged also if you would tell me whether you think some rules might not be passed (though not promulgated) for pensioning or endowing with lands native public servants of extraordinary merit, as well as of pensioning all who accomplished a certain period of service.

'I have had none of your Minutes for a long time; and, as I do not know your present private secretary, I do not know how to apply for a proper selection; but I set a high value on those I have received, and should be very thankful if the supply could be continued [1].'

In 1822 Munro directed the Board of Revenue to ascertain the number of schools and the state of education among the natives in the provinces, and after receipt of the reports from the collectors, he summarized and remarked on the Board's review. The main causes of the low state of education he considered to be the little encouragement which it received

[1] Colebrooke's *Life*, ii. 142.

from there being but little demand for it, and the poverty of the people; but these difficulties might be surmounted by good education being rendered more easy and general, and by the preference which would be given to well-educated men in all public offices. He therefore authorized a grant to the Madras School Book Society for educating teachers, and directed the establishment in each Collectorate of two principal schools, one for Hindus and one for Muhammadans, and one for each Tâluk; the monthly salaries of the teachers were to be only Rs. 15 and Rs. 9, but as each schoolmaster would get as much more from his scholars 'his situation will probably be better than that of a parish schoolmaster in Scotland.' 'Whatever expense,' he wrote, 'Government may incur in the education of the people will be amply repaid by the improvement of the country, for the general diffusion of knowledge is inseparably followed by more orderly habits, by increasing industry, by a taste for the comforts of life, by exertions to acquire them, and by the growing prosperity of the people.'

CHAPTER XIV

The Burmese War, 1824–1826

Though complete peace reigned throughout the Madras Presidency during Munro's tenure of office—as indeed may be said to have been the case ever since—it included one of the most important events in the history of British India—the first Burmese war, 1824–1826. The Burmese had taken possession of the island of Sháhpuri off the coast of Chittagong, overrun Assam, and made a series of encroachments on the British Districts of Bengal. War was declared by the Governor-General, Lord Amherst, on February 24, 1824, but it was not till the 23rd of that month that the Government of Madras learned that war was even impending on being informed that that Presidency would be required to furnish the native branch of the force.

Writing to the Duke of Wellington, Munro said that in the previous September (1823) he had sent a letter to the Court of Directors asking to be relieved; he had been long enough in India, and as everything was quiet and settling in good order he thought it a proper time for leaving; had he suspected that in a few months there was to be both war and famine he should never have thought of resigning until our difficulties were at an end. 'I was probably,' he says, 'more surprised at hearing of the intended war than people will be at home, for I had not the least suspicion that we were to go to war with the King of Ava till a letter reached this Presidency in February last, asking us what number of troops we could furnish for foreign service.'

On February 25, 1824, Munro wrote to Lord Amherst stating what Madras could do. 'Our troops,' he said, 'lie convenient, and they are eager to be employed. I am no less anxious that they should go wherever there is service, but I wish at the same time that they should go with every means to guard against failure. A service of this kind requires more than any other that every equipment should be ample, because there can seldom be any medium between complete success and failure, partial success is little better than an expensive failure.' Lord Amherst at once replied seeking Munro's advice, stating that the matters on which he had already written were 'far beyond the reach of his experience,' and that he 'might rely upon frequent communications from his Government upon all matters connected with the measures in contemplation.'

A constant correspondence was kept up between the Governor-General and Munro, whose long experience of Indian warfare and knowledge of Asiatic character enabled him to be a wise counsellor, in addition to his indefatigable exertions in seeing to the despatch of troops, boats, transport, bullocks, and supplies; at the same time he took precautions that there should be neither an outbreak nor the fear of it owing to the Presidency being almost denuded of troops.

Writing to Munro on April 22, 1824, Lord Amherst informed Munro of the conditions of peace to be offered to the Burmese, as soon as Rangoon should be taken:—

'We have no wish to weaken or dismember the Burmese Empire, nor to acquire for ourselves any extension of the territory we already possess. We purpose to require that the Burmese should relinquish their newly-acquired possessions in Assam, from whence they have the means of descending the Brahmaputra, and overrunning our provinces at a season of the year when our troops cannot keep the field; that they should renounce the right of interference in the independent countries of Cachar; that the boundary between Chittagong and Arakan should be accurately defined; and finally, that they should pay the expenses, or a share of the expenses, of the war in which they have compelled us to engage. These conditions, with the addition, possibly, of a stipulation respecting the *independence of Manipur*, we are, I think, entitled to demand.'

The following extract from a letter from Munro to Mr. Sulivan, dated July 11, 1825, gives his views on the progress of the war up to that date:—

'The original plan of the invasion of Ava was romantic and visionary, and was, I believe, suggested by Captain Canning. It was that Sir A. Campbell, after occupying Rangoon and collecting a sufficient number of boats, should, with the help of the south-west wind, proceed against the stream to Amarápura at once. This, even if it had been practicable, was too hazardous, as it would have exposed the whole force to destruction, from the intercepting of its supplies. Had there been boats enough, this scheme might have been partially executed with great advantage, by going up the river as high as Sarawa. This would have given us the command of the delta, and of the navigation of all the branches of the Irawadi, and would have saved the troops from much of the privations which they have suffered from being shut up at Rangoon. But even if there had been a sufficient number of boats, Sir A. Campbell would have been justified, by our ignorance of the country and of the enemy, in not making the attempt until he should have received more troops, to leave detachments at different places on the river, to keep open his communications with Rangoon.

'When Captain Canning's plan of sailing up to the capital was abandoned, two others were thought of, but both were impracticable: one was to proceed in the dry season by land from Pegu; the other was to re-embark the troops, land somewhere on the coast of Arakan, and march from thence through the hills to the Irawadi. This Government, from its subordinate situation, has of course nothing to say in the plans of foreign war; but I took advantage of a private correspondence with which I have been honoured by Lord

Amherst, to state privately my opinion strongly against both plans. I said that re-embarkation would be attended with the most disgraceful and disastrous consequences; that the measure would be supposed to have proceeded from fear; that it would encourage the enemy, and would deter the people of the country wherever we might again land, from coming near us, or bringing us provisions for sale; that we knew nothing of the coast of Arakan or the interior; that if the troops landed there, they would be in greater distress than at Rangoon, because they would find less rice, and be as much exposed to the weather; that they could not possibly penetrate into the country without carriage cattle, of which they had none; and that they would be at last compelled to re-embark again without effecting anything. I said that the nature of the country, and the difficulty of sending draught and carriage cattle by sea, pointed out clearly that our main line of operations could only be by the course of the Irawadi, partly by land[1] and partly by water, and that this would give us the double advantage of passing through the richest part of the enemy's country, and of cutting off his communication with it whenever we got above the point where the branches separate from the main stream of the Irawadi.

'I calculated that if Sir A. Campbell adopted this plan, he would reach Prome before the rains; and that when they were over, he would be able to con-

[1] He had recommended that the Bengal troops should advance by Manipur.

tinue his march to Amarápura. When I reckoned on his getting no farther than Prome this season, I had not so low an opinion of the Burman troops as I now have. I was induced to form a very low estimate of their military character, from their cautious and irresolute operations against the detachment at Rámu, in May, 1824; and from all their subsequent conduct they appear to be very inferior in military spirit to any of the nations of India. There were no letters from Prome later than the 6th of June; the monsoon had set in, and everything in the neighbourhood was quiet. The heads of districts had submitted, and were sending in supplies. It was expected that offers of peace would be sent from Ava as soon as the occupation of Prome should be known. It is difficult to say what such a government will do; it may submit to our terms or reject them; but we ought to be prepared to ensure them by advancing to Amarápura, and, if necessary, dismembering the empire, and restoring the Pegu nation. If we encouraged them, a leader would probably be found, and we might, without committing ourselves to protect him hereafter, make him strong enough, before we left the country, to maintain himself against the broken power of Ava.

'We have sent on foreign service beyond sea, from Madras, five regiments of European infantry, fourteen regiments of Native infantry, two companies of European artillery, a battalion of pioneers, and above one thousand dooly bearers, and we have relieved the Bengal subsidiary force at Nágpur. The rest of our troops are thinly scattered over a great extent of country, and will have very severe duty until those on foreign service return. We are obliged to be more careful than in ordinary times; but I see no reason to apprehend any serious commotion, or anything beyond the occasional disturbances of poligars, which we are seldom for any long time ever entirely free from in this country. I confess I cannot understand what the Bengal Government want to do with so many additional troops, or with any addition at all. Mr. Adam left them quite enough, and more than enough, to carry on the Burman war and to protect their own territory. They have not sent a single Native regiment beyond sea, except a marine battalion; they have in Arakan and their eastern frontier twelve or thirteen Native regiments more than formerly; but they have got nine of them by troops at Nágpur and Mhow having been relieved from Madras and Bombay, while these troops, which have moved to the eastward, still cover the country from which they were drawn. We had once five battalions in the Bárámahal; we have one there now—the whole have been advanced to the Ceded Districts. The military authorities in Bengal seem to think that when troops are drawn together in large bodies in time of war, new levies must always be made to occupy the stations from which troops have been taken to join the large body. If we follow such a principle, there can be no limit to the increase of our armies. I found much inconvenience from its adoption in Bengal, because the increase of the Bengal army is narrowly observed by the armies of the other Presidencies, and raises expectations which cannot be satisfied.'

At the conclusion of the war Munro thus expressed his views on the peace and as to what should have been done in a letter to the Duke of Wellington, dated April 16, 1826:—

'I did not think of troubling you with another letter; but as we have at last made peace with the Burmans, I think I may as well give you a few lines by way of finishing the war. I mentioned in my last what kind of troops the Burman armies were composed of, so that it is not necessary to say anything more of them, except that they did not improve in the progress of the war. We are well out of this war. There have been so many projects since it commenced, that I scarcely expected ever to see any one plan pursued consistently. There has been no want of energy or decision at any time in attacking the enemy; but there has certainly been a great want of many of the arrangements and combinations by which the movements of an army are facilitated, and its success rendered more certain. There were, no doubt, great difficulties: everything was new; the country was difficult, and the climate was destructive; but still, more enterprise in exploring the routes and passes on some occasions, and more foresight in others in ascertaining in time the means of conveyance and subsistence, and what was practicable and what was not, would have saved much time.

'We are chiefly indebted for peace to Lord Amherst's judgment and firmness in persevering in offensive operations, in spite of all arguments in favour of a defensive war, founded upon idle alarms about the power of the Burmans, and the danger of advancing to so great a distance as the capital. Had he given way, and directed Sir A. Campbell to amuse himself with a defensive system about Prome or Meaday, we should have had no peace for another campaign or two. Every object that could have been expected from the war has been attained. We took what we wanted, and the enemy would have given up whatever we desired, had it been twice as much. They have been so dispirited, and our position in Arakan and Martaban gives us such ready access to the Irawadi, that I hardly think they will venture to go to war with us again. The Tennasserim coast cannot at present pay the expense of defending it; it may possibly do so in a few years, as its resources will, no doubt, improve in our hands, and there may be commercial advantages that may make up for its deficiency of territorial revenue. I should have liked better to have taken nothing for ourselves in that quarter, but to have made Pegu independent, with Tennasserim attached to it.

'Within two months after our landing at Rangoon, when it was ascertained that the Court of Ava would not treat, I would have set to work to emancipate Pegu; and, had we done so, it would have been in a condition to protect itself; but to make this still more sure, I would have left a corps of about six thousand men in the country until their government and military force were properly organized; five or six years would have been fully sufficient for these objects, and we could then have gradually withdrawn the whole of our force. We should by this plan have had only a temporary establishment in Pegu, the expense of which would have been chiefly, if not wholly, paid by that country; whereas the expense of Tennasserim will, with fortifications, be as great as that of Pegu, and will be permanent, and will not give us the advantage of having a friendly native power to counterbalance Ava. Pegu is so fertile, and has so many natural advantages, that it would in a few years have been a more powerful state than Ava.

'One principal reason in favour of separating Pegu was the great difficulty and slowness with which all our operations must have proceeded, had the country been hostile, and if the Burman commanders knew how to avail themselves properly of this spirit, and the risk of total failure from our inability to protect our supplies upon our long line of communication. The Bengal Government were however always averse to the separation of Pegu; they thought that the Burmans and Peguers were completely amalgamated into one people; that the Peguers had no wish for independence; that if they had, there was no prince remaining of their dynasty, nor even any chief of commanding influence, to assume the government;

that it would retard the attainment of peace; that the project was, in fact, impracticable; and that if even practicable, the execution of it was not desirable, as it would involve us for ever in Indo-Chinese politics, by the necessity of protecting Pegu. Even if we had been obliged to keep troops for an unlimited time in Pegu, it would have saved the necessity of keeping an additional force on the eastern unhealthy frontier of Bengal, as the Burmans would never have disturbed Bengal while we were in Pegu. The Bengal Government were, no doubt, right in being cautious. They acted upon the best, though imperfect, information they possessed.

'Those who have the responsibility cannot be expected to be so adventurous as we who have none. But I believe that there is no man who is not now convinced that the Taliens (Peguers) deserted the Burman Government, sought independence, and in the hope of obtaining it, though without any pledge on our part, aided in supplying all our wants with a zeal which could not have been surpassed by our subjects.

'We sent to Rangoon about three thousand five hundred draught and carriage bullocks; and could have sent five times as many, had there been tonnage.'

In June, 1825, Sir Thomas Munro's services were rewarded by his elevation to a Baronetcy of the United Kingdom, and at the same time it was under the consideration of the authorities at home to appoint him to the Governor-Generalship when it should fall vacant; but, as he wrote to a friend in the India Office, it was now too late: 'I am like an overworked horse and require a little rest. Ever since I came to this Government almost every paper of any importance has been written by myself, and during the whole course of the Burman war, though little of my writing appears, I have been incessantly engaged in discussions and inquiries and correspondence, all connected with the objects of the war, though, from not being official, they cannot appear on record. Were I to go to Bengal I could hardly hold out two years. . . . I never wish to remain in office when I feel that I cannot do justice to it.'

On April 11, 1826, the Governor-General in Council wrote to Sir Thomas expressing the 'heartfelt obligations' of the Government of India 'for the ever-active and cordial co-operation of the Madras Government in the conduct of the war,' and stating that 'to the extraordinary exertions of your Government we are mainly indebted for the prosecution of the Burmese war to the successful issue which, under Providence, has crowned our arms.' In Nov. 1826 the Court of Directors passed the following resolution: 'Resolved unanimously, That the thanks of this Court be given to Major-General Sir Thomas Munro, Bart., K.C.B., for the alacrity, zeal, perseverance and forecast which he so signally manifested throughout the whole course of the late war, in contributing all the available resources of the Madras Government towards bringing it to a successful termination.' And in the House of Lords, Lord Goderich declared that it was 'impossible for any one to form an adequate idea of the efforts made by Sir Thomas Munro at the head of the Madras Government.'

CHAPTER XV

Last Tours and Death

Though no Governor of Madras came to the office with such a thorough knowledge of the country, few, if any, before or since, have made so extensive and prolonged tours throughout the Presidency as Munro did. Recent Governors of Madras have in the course of frequent tours visited every District in the Presidency, and even in the hottest seasons of the year have set an example to district officers when in times of famine or other difficulties the presence of the head of the Government was likely to inspire zeal on the part of officials and confidence in the hearts of the people. But this has been done with the help of the railways, now forming a network all over the country; while in Munro's tours he 'marched every day, except when obliged to halt by the rising of rivers or the necessity of giving rest to the cattle.'

In the autumn of 1822 he made a tour which lasted three months, through Nellore and the Northern Circárs, i.e. from Madras to the Gúmsúr Hills in Ganjám, and left on record a long and most interesting Minute describing his tour and his interviews with the zamindárs (of whom he saw all but two), the Rájás of Vizianagram, Venkatagiri, and Kálahasti, and embodying in it the result of his observations and views, many of which have been rendered additionally interesting by incidents that have occurred in recent years in the places he visited. In 1821 he visited the Báramahal, 'both for the purpose of seeing the inhabitants and making some inquiries into the state of the country, and of revisiting scenes where above thirty years before he had spent seven very happy years.'

In 1823 he made a tour through the Ceded Districts; he was glad to get away from Cuddapah, with 'the thermometer at 94 and its dry parching wind,' but he adds: 'I still like this country, notwithstanding its heat; it is full of industrious cultivators, and I like to recognize among them a great number of my old acquaintances, who, I hope, are as glad to see me as I them.'

In 1826 Sir Thomas Munro renewed his application to be relieved of the governorship, and looked forward to the arrival of his successor early in the following year. Lady Munro, however, was obliged to leave for Europe before he could accompany her, as the illness of their second son, Campbell Munro, who had been born in September, 1823, rendered an immediate departure from India the sole chance of saving the child's life. Lady Munro left Madras in

March, 1826, but they never met again, it being the fate of Sir Thomas, like that of many another Anglo-Indian, to be buried in the land to which he had given the best part of his life within a twelvemonth of the time when he hoped to return to the country of his birth.

In the autumn of 1826 Sir Thomas Munro made a tour through the Districts of Chengalpat, South Arcot, Tanjore, Trichinopoli, Madura, Tinnevelli, and Coimbatore, and thence up to the Nílgiris. From Ootacamund in September he wrote to his wife a description of those then little-known mountains which, when published in Gleig's *Life*, was one of the first accounts that appeared in print of those Hills and the sweet 'half-English Nílgiri air.'

After leaving the Nílgiris, on his way to Madras *viâ* Bangalore, Munro visited the Falls of the Káveri, which he thus describes: 'They are very grand, and rather exceeded than fell short of my expectations. The fall on the southern branch of the river is about a mile below that on the northern which we visited together. It is something in the form of a horse-shoe, and consists of seven streams falling from the same level, and divided only from each other by fragments of the rock. There is a descent to the bed of the river by steps; and when you stand there, nearly surrounded by cataracts covering you with small rain, and look at the great breadth of the whole fall, and the woody hills rising behind it, the scene appears very wild and magnificent.'

To Munro's great disappointment a delay occurred

in the appointment of his successor, and as he could not be relieved before October, he decided on paying a farewell visit to the Ceded Districts, and set out from Madras towards the end of May, 1827.

A legend survives in various forms with reference to his journey through the Cuddapah District. One version is that, while riding through a narrow gorge, where the Pápaghni breaks through the hills, Munro suddenly looked up at the steep cliffs above, and then said, 'What a beautiful garland of flowers they have stretched across the valley!' His companions all looked, but said they could see nothing. 'Why, there it is,' said he, 'all made of gold.' Again they looked, and saw nothing: but one of his old native servants said, 'Alas! a great and good man will soon die!'

After halting some time at Anantápur, the Governor and his party reached Gooty on July 4. Here several sepoys were carried off by cholera; on the following morning the camp was moved, and on the 6th the party reached Pattikonda, in the Karnúl District, twenty-two miles from Gooty. A few hours after their arrival, Sir Thomas himself was attacked with cholera; the symptoms were at first not alarming, and in the middle of the day hopes were entertained of his recovery. During one of his rallies he exclaimed, in a tone of peculiar sweetness, that it was 'almost worth while to be ill in order to be so kindly nursed[1].' In the

[1] Among those about Sir Thomas Munro at the time of his death was a lad named Henry Bower, afterwards a well-known missionary and Tamil scholar.

evening he grew worse, and at about half-past nine on the night of July 6, 1827, he calmly passed away.

His remains were at once carried to Gooty and buried in the English graveyard there—a most picturesque spot at the foot of the great Gooty rock and fortress which towers above. The tomb, a flat slab with a brief inscription and railed in, is still carefully seen to. In April, 1831, his remains were removed to Madras, and interred just in front of the Governor's pew in St. Mary's Church, Fort St. George; and close by is a mural tablet with a bust of Sir Thomas erected by his widow.

The news of Munro's death was received in Madras with feelings of deep regret by all classes. The Government issued a Gazette extraordinary on July 9, in which occurs the following passage: 'His sound and vigorous understanding, his transcendent talents, his indefatigable application, his varied stores of knowledge, his attainments as an Oriental scholar, his intimate acquaintance with the habits and feelings of the native soldiers and inhabitants generally, his patience, temper, facility of access, and kindness of manner, would have ensured him distinction in any line of employment. These qualities were admirably adapted to the duties which he had to perform in organizing the resources, and establishing the tranquillity of those provinces where his latest breath has been drawn, and where he had long been known by the appellation of the *Father* of the People.'

A public meeting was without delay held in Madras, at which resolutions were passed expressing the regret of those assembled of all classes in the community at 'the calamity which has occurred in the death of our late revered Governor,' and 'the pride they took in his fame'; that his justice, benevolence, frankness, and hospitality were no less conspicuous than the extraordinary faculties of his mind; and that a subscription be opened to erect a statue to his memory.

At Pattikonda Government caused a grove of trees to be planted and a well or tank with stone steps to be constructed near the spot where he died; and at Gooty a similar well and a large choultry or rest-house for native travellers were constructed, and for several years food was distributed gratuitously in his honour at it; within the 'Munro choultry' is hung a copy of the large full-length portrait of Munro by Sir Martin Shee, copies of which also adorn the walls of the cutcherry at Bellary and other public buildings in the Ceded Districts, and the Revenue Board Office, Madras.

It was not till 1839 that the equestrian statue of Munro by Sir Francis Chantrey arrived at Madras, and on October 23 of that year it was exposed to public view with all due ceremony, after having been erected in one of the most conspicuous sites in Madras.

Lady Munro survived her husband twenty-three years, dying in 1850. Both of Sir Thomas' sons are still living. The eldest, the present Sir Thomas Munro, was formerly a captain in the 10th Hussars, and is unmarried; the second son, Mr. Campbell Munro, formerly a Captain in the Grenadier Guards, has had nine children, the third of whom, Philip Harvey Munro, Lieut. R. N., born in 1866, was lost in H.M.S. *Victoria* on the 22nd June, 1893.

APPENDIX

MEMORANDUM OF THE SERVICES OF SIR T. MUNRO,

WRITTEN BY HIMSELF.

[*The original orthography is retained.*]

'I ARRIVED at Madras on the 15th of January, 1780, and did duty in the garrison of Fort St. George until the invasion of the Carnatic, in July, by Hyder.

I marched on the —— with the grenadier company to which I belonged, the 21st battalion of Sepoys, and a detachment of artillery, to Poonamallee[1]; and from thence, after being joined by His Majesty's 73rd regiment, to the Mount[2], where the army had been ordered to assemble. The cadet company having arrived in camp, I was ordered to do duty with it on the 20th of August, 1780, and marched on the 26th of that month with the army under Lieutenant-General Sir Hector Munro. I continued with the army while it was commanded by that officer, and afterwards by Lieutenant-General Sir Eyre Coote and Lieutenant-General Stewart, during all the operations in the Carnatic, in the war with the Mysoreans and the French, from the commencement of hostilities by Hyder Ally, until the cessation of arms with the French, on the 2nd of July, 1783.

I was present at the retreat of Sir Hector Munro from Conjeveram[3] to Madras, after the defeat of Colonel Bailie by Hyder Ally on the 10th of September, 1780[4].

[1] About thirteen miles south-west of Madras.

[2] St. Thomas's Mount, eight miles south of Madras.

[3] In South Arcot.

[4] See p. 19.

I was with the army under Sir Eyre Coote, at the relief of Wandiwash[1], on the 24th of January, 1781. At the cannonade by Hyder Ally, on the march from Pondicherry to Cuddalore[2], on the 7th of February, 1781. At the assault of Chidambaram[2], 18th of June, 1781. At the battle of Porto Novo[2], 1st of July, 1781. At the siege of Tripassore[3], 22nd of August, 1781. At the battle of Pollilore[3], 27th of August, 1781. At the battle of Sholinghur[1], 27th of September, 1781.

I was with the advanced division of the army, under Colonel Owen, when that officer was attacked and defeated by Hyder Ally, near Chittoor[1], on the 23rd of October, 1781; but the 16th battalion of Sepoys, to which I belonged, having been detached to the village of Magraul, about five miles distant, to collect grain, and a body of the enemy having thrown itself between this post and the corps under Colonel Owen, and rendered the junction of the battalions impracticable, Captain Cox, who commanded it, made good his retreat to the main army by a forced march of nearly forty miles over the hills.

I was present at the taking of Chittoor on the 11th of November, 1781. On the — of November, 1781, having been appointed quartermaster of brigade, I joined the 5th, or left, brigade of the army. I was present when the army, on its march to relieve Vellore[1], was harrassed and cannonaded by Hyder Ally on the 10th and 13th of January, 1782. I was present at the battle of Arni[1] on the 2nd of June, 1782. At the attack of the French lines and battle of Cuddalore, on the 13th of June, 1783; on which occasion I acted as aid-de-camp to Major Cotgrave, field-officer of the day, who commanded the centre attack.

[1] In North Arcot. [2] In South Arcot.
[3] In Chengalpat District.

I was present at the siege of Cuddalore until the 2nd of July, 1783, when hostilities ceased, in consequence of accounts having been received of the peace with France. From this period I remained with a division of the army cantoned in the neighbourhood of Madras, until after the definitive treaty with Tippu Sultan, in March, 1784.

In July, 1784, I proceeded to join my corps stationed at Melloor, near Madura. In January 1785, having been removed to the 30th battalion, I joined it at Tanjore; and on its being reduced a few months after, I was appointed to the 1st battalion of Sepoys, in the same garrison, with which I did duty until —— 1786, when, being promoted to the rank of Lieutenant, I was appointed to the —— battalion European infantry[1], in garrison at Madras.

In 1786 I was removed to the 11th battalion, and joined it in September, at Cassimcottah, near Vizagapatam. In January, 1787, having been appointed to the 21st battalion, I joined it in the following month at Vellore.

In August, 1788, having been appointed an assistant in the Intelligence Department, under Captain Read, and attached to the headquarters of the force destined to take possession of the province of Guntoor[2], ceded by the Soubah of the Deccan, I joined the force assembled near Ongole[3] for that purpose, and continued with it until, the service having been completed by the occupation of the forts, I proceeded to Ambore, a frontier station, commanded by Captain Read, under whom I was employed in the Intelligence Department until October, 1790; in that month I joined the 21st battalion of Native infantry in the army under Colonel Maxwell, which, in consequence of the war with Tippu Sultan, invaded the Barmahal.

[1] The Madras European Regiment. [2] In the Kistna District.
[3] In Villore District.

I was with the detachment sent out to cover the retreat of the 1st regiment of Native cavalry, which fell into an ambuscade near Caveripatam[1], on the 11th of November, 1790. I served in the field with the main army, or with detachments of it, until the conclusion of the war.

I was present in the pursuit of Tippoo by Lieutenant-General Meadows, through the Topoor Pass[1], on the 18th of November, 1790.

When the army under Lord Cornwallis entered Mysore in February, 1791, I was appointed to the command of a small body of two hundred Sepoys, called the Prize Guard, to be employed in securing captured property and in collecting cattle for the army on its march, and various other duties.

I was stationed in the town of Bangalore during the siege of the fort, and was present when it was taken by storm, on the 21st of March, 1791.

I was with the army at the battle of Karigal, near Seringapatam, on the 15th of May, 1791.

On the return of the army from Seringapatam to the neighbourhood of Bangalore, I was constantly employed on detachment in escorting military stores and provisions to camp until December, 1791, when, the army being ready to advance to the siege of Seringapatam, I was thrown into the fort of Cootradroog to cover the march of convoys from Bangalore to camp.

In the following month, January 1792, I was appointed assistant to Captain Read, who commanded a detachment at Bangalore, employed in forwarding supplies to the army.

In February, 1792, I marched with this officer and joined the army before Seringapatam during the negotiations for peace. On the settlement of the peace, in March, 1792, I marched with the detachment in charge of the two sons of Tippoo, who were to be sent as hostages to Madras.

[1] In Salem District.

In April, 1792, I marched with the force ordered to occupy the Baramahal, ceded by Tippoo to the British Government.

From April, 1792, until March, 1799, I was employed in the civil administration of that country.

On the breaking out of the war with Tippoo Sultan, I joined the army under Lieutenant-General Harris, intended for the siege of Seringapatam, near Royacottah[1], on the 5th of March, 1799. Colonel Read, to whom I had been appointed secretary, having been detached on the 11th to bring forward the supplies in the rear of the army, took the hill-fort of Shulagherry[1] by assault on the 15th, on which occasion I was present. The detachment, after collecting the convoys, set out for Seringapatam; but owing to the labour of repairing the pass of Caveripuram[2], it did not reach the army until the 10th of May, six days after the fall of the place.

Having been appointed by the Governor-General, Lord Mornington, one of the Secretaries to the Commission for the settlement of Mysore, I acted in that capacity until the conclusion of the Partition Treaty and the installation of the Rajah, on the — of July, 1799.

As I had been appointed to the charge of the civil administration of Canara, I entered that province in the end of July, and joined the force which had been previously sent to expel the enemy's garrisons. From July, 1799, till the end of October, 1800, I remained in charge of Canara.

In the beginning of November, 1800, I proceeded to the Ceded Districts, to the civil administration of which I had been appointed in the preceding month. I continued in charge of the Ceded Districts until the 23rd of October, 1807, when I sailed for England, having then been employed, without interruption, during a period of twenty-eight years in India.

I remained in England from April, 1808, till May, 1814,

[1] In Salem District. [2] In Coimbatore.

when I embarked for India, and reached Madras on the 16th of September, 1814.

From September, 1814, till July, 1817, I was employed as Principal Commissioner for the revision of the internal administration in the Madras territories.

When preparations were made for taking the field against the Pindarries I was appointed to the command of the reserve of the army, under Lieutenant-General Sir Thomas Hislop. The reserve was, in July 1817, ordered to advance and take possession of Dharwar, which the Peishwah had ceded to the British Government by the Treaty of Poonah. I reached Dharwar on the 10th of August, three days after it had been given up to the advanced battalion of the reserve. I remained at Dharwar until the 11th of October, engaged in arranging with Mahratta Commissioners the limits of the districts which had been ceded by the Peishwah. On the 12th of October I commenced my march for Sundoor, a district held by a refractory Mahratta chief, whom I was ordered to dispossess and deliver it up to the officers of the Peishwah.

On the — of October I arrived at Sundoor, which the chief surrendered without opposition. On the 7th of November, 1817, having repassed the Toombuddra, I directed the reserve, in pursuance of orders from headquarters, to take up a position beyond the Kistna, under Brigadier-General Pritzler, and proceeded myself to Dharwar to finish the political arrangements with the Mahratta Commissioners.

On the 14th of November arrive at Dharwar; learn that the Peishwah has commenced hostilities, and, finding that my rejoining the reserve was rendered impracticable by the interposition of the enemy's troops, determine to endeavour to subdue the neighbouring districts by the influence of a party among the leading inhabitants, and by the aid of a detachment from the garrison of Dharwar, assisted by a body of irregulars collected from the country.

On the — of December, 1817, disperse a body of the enemy's horse, joined by the garrison of Nawlgoond, and take possession of the forts evacuated by the enemy on our approach. On the — of January, 1818, having been joined by a small battering-train from Bellary, lay siege to Guddur, which surrenders on the — of January. On the — of January take the fort of Dumbull. On the — of January the fort of Hoobli, and on the day following its dependent fort of Misriekottah is given up to a detachment sent to occupy it. On the — of February, 1818, pass the Malpurbah; and after routing a body of the enemy's horse and foot near the village of ——, encamped near Badami. On the 17th of February, a practicable breach having been made, storm and carry the place. On the 21st of February take Bagricottah. On the 10th of February take Padshapoor.

On the 21st of March encamp before Belgaum; and, after a siege of twenty days, take the place by capitulation on the 10th of April. On the 16th of April, Kalla Nundilghur is given up to a detachment of irregulars which I sent to invest it. On the 22nd of April rejoin the reserve.

On the 10th of May take the pettah of Sholapur by assault. Defeat the Peishwah's infantry under Gunput Row at the battle of Sholapur. 15th of May, take the fort of Sholapur by capitulation after a practicable breach had been made. 31st of May, encamp before Nepauni and compel Appah Dessay to give orders for the delivery of Wokarah and other places to the Rajah of Bolapoor.

On the 8th of August, 1818, having received the surrender of Paurghur, the last fort held for the Peishwah, resign my command, after having, in the course of the campaign, reduced all the Peishwah's territories between the Toombuddra and Kistna, and from the Kistna northward to Akloos, on the Neemah, and eastward to the Nizam's frontier.'

INDEX

THE END.

RULERS OF INDIA:

THE CLARENDON PRESS SERIES OF INDIAN HISTORICAL RETROSPECTS.

Edited by SIR W. W. HUNTER, K.C.S.I., C.I.E.

Price 2s. 6d. each.

The following volumes have been arranged for up to January, 1894:—

I. *AKBAR: and the Rise of the Mughal Empire*, by COLONEL MALLESON, C.S.I., Author of *A History of the Indian Mutiny; The History of Afghanistan; Herat, &c.* [Published.] Fourth thousand.

II. *ALBUQUERQUE: and the Early Portuguese Settlements in India*, by H. MORSE STEPHENS, Esq., M.A., Balliol College, Lecturer on Indian History at Cambridge, Author of *The French Revolution; The Story of Portugal, &c.* [Published.]

III. *AURANGZÍB: and the Decay of the Mughal Empire*, by STANLEY LANE POOLE, Esq., B.A., Author of *The Coins of the Mughal Emperors; The Life of Stratford Canning; Catalogue of Indian Coins in the British Museum, &c.* [Published.]

IV. *MADHAVA RAO SINDHIA: and the Hindú Reconquest of India*, by H. G. KEENE, Esq., M.A., C.I.E., Author of *The Moghul Empire, &c.* [Published.]

V. *LORD CLIVE: and the Establishment of the English in India*, by COLONEL MALLESON, C.S.I. [Published.]

VI. *DUPLEIX: and the Struggle for India by the European Nations*, by COLONEL MALLESON, C.S.I., Author of *The History of the French in India, &c.* [Published.] Third thousand.

VII. *WARREN HASTINGS: and the Founding of the British Administration*, by CAPTAIN L. J. TROTTER, Author of *India under Victoria, &c.* [Published.] Third thousand.

VIII. *THE MARQUESS CORNWALLIS: and the Consolidation of British Rule*, by W. S. SETON-KARR, Esq., sometime Foreign Secretary to the Government of India, Author of *Selections from the Calcutta Gazettes*, 3 vols. (1784–1805). [Published.] Third thousand.

IX. *HAIDAR ALÍ AND TIPÚ SULTÁN: and the Struggle with the Muhammadan Powers of the South*, by LEWIN BENTHAM BOWRING, Esq., C.S.I., sometime Private Secretary to the Viceroy (Lord Canning) and Chief Commissioner of Mysore. Author of *Eastern Experiences.* [Published.]

X. *THE MARQUESS WELLESLEY: and the Development of the Company into the Supreme Power in India*, by the Rev. W. H. HUTTON, M.A., Fellow and Tutor of St. John's College, Oxford. [Published.]

XI. *THE MARQUESS OF HASTINGS: and the Final Overthrow of the Maráthá Power*, by MAJOR ROSS OF BLADENSBURG, C.B., Coldstream Guards; F.R.G.S. [Published.]

XII. *MOUNTSTUART ELPHINSTONE: and the Making of South-Western India*, by J. S. COTTON, Esq., M.A., formerly Fellow of Queen's College, Oxford, Author of *The Decennial Statement of the Moral and Material Progress and Condition of India*, presented to Parliament (1885), &c. [Published.]

XIII. *SIR THOMAS MUNRO: and the British Settlement of the Madras Presidency*, by JOHN BRADSHAW, Esq., M.A., LL.D., Inspector of Schools, Madras. [Published.]

XIV. *EARL AMHERST: and the British Advance eastwards to Burma*, chiefly from unpublished papers of the Amherst family, by Mrs. ANNE THACKERAY RITCHIE, Author of *Old Kensington, &c.*, assisted by RICHARDSON EVANS, Esq. [Shortly.]

XV. *LORD WILLIAM BENTINCK: and the Company as a Governing and Non-trading Power*, by DEMETRIUS BOULGER, Esq., Author of *England and Russia in Central Asia; The History of China, &c.* [Published.]

XVI *EARL OF AUCKLAND: and the First Afghan War*, by CAPTAIN L. J. TROTTER, Author of *India under Victoria, &c.* [Published.]

XVII. *VISCOUNT HARDINGE: and the Advance of the British Dominions into the Punjab*, by his Son and Private Secretary, the Right Hon. VISCOUNT HARDINGE. [Published.] Third thousand.

XVIII. *RANJIT SINGH: and the Sikh Barrier between our Growing Empire and Central Asia*, by SIR LEPEL GRIFFIN, K.C.S.I., Author of *The Punjab Chiefs, &c.* [Published.] Third thousand.

XIX. *THE MARQUESS OF DALHOUSIE: and the Final Development of the Company's Rule*, by SIR WILLIAM WILSON HUNTER, K.C.S.I., M.A. [Published.] Fifth thousand.

XX. *CLYDE AND STRATHNAIRN: and the Suppression of the Great Revolt*, by MAJOR-GENERAL SIR OWEN TUDOR BURNE, K.C.S.I., sometime Military Secretary to the Commander-in-Chief in India. [Published.] Third thousand.

XXI. *EARL CANNING: and the Transfer of India from the Company to the Crown*, by SIR HENRY S. CUNNINGHAM, K.C.I.E., M.A., Author of *British India and its Rulers, &c.* [Published.] Third thousand.

XXII. *LORD LAWRENCE: and the Reconstruction of India under the Crown*, by SIR CHARLES UMPHERSTON AITCHISON, K.C.S.I., LL.D., formerly Foreign Secretary to the Government of India, and late Lieutenant-Governor of the Punjab. [Published.]

XXIII. *THE EARL OF MAYO: and the Consolidation of the Queen's Rule in India*, by SIR WILLIAM WILSON HUNTER, K.C.S.I., M.A., LL.D. [Published.] Third thousand.

SUPPLEMENTARY VOLUMES.

A BRIEF HISTORY OF THE INDIAN PEOPLES, by SIR WILLIAM WILSON HUNTER, K.C.S.I. Twentieth Edition; 78th thousand. Price 3*s.* 6*d.* [Published.]

JAMES THOMASON: and the British Settlement of North-Western India, by SIR RICHARD TEMPLE, Bart., M.P., formerly Lieutenant-Governor of Bengal, and Governor of Bombay. Price 3*s.* 6*d.* [Published.]

Opinions of the Press

ON

SIR WILLIAM HUNTER'S 'DALHOUSIE.'

'An interesting and exceedingly readable volume. . . . . Sir William Hunter has produced a valuable work about an important epoch in English history in India, and he has given us a pleasing insight into the character of a remarkable Englishman. The "Rulers of India" series, which he has initiated, thus makes a successful beginning in his hands with one who ranks among the greatest of the great names which will be associated with the subject.'—*The Times.*

'To no one is the credit for the improved condition of public intelligence [regarding India] more due than to Sir William Hunter. From the beginning of his career as an Indian Civilian he has devoted a rare literary faculty to the task of enlightening his countrymen on the subject of England's greatest dependency. . . . By inspiring a small army of fellow-labourers with his own spirit, by inducing them to conform to his own method, and shaping a huge agglomeration of facts into a lucid and intelligible system, Sir W. Hunter has brought India and its innumerable interests within the pale of achievable knowledge, and has given definite shape to the truths which its history establishes and the problems which it suggests. . . . Such contributions to literature are apt to be taken as a matter of course, because their highest merit is to conceal the labour, and skill, and knowledge involved in their production; but they raise the whole level of public intelligence, and generate an atmosphere in which the baleful influences of folly, ignorance, prejudice, and presumption dwindle and disappear.'—*Saturday Review.*

'Admirably calculated to impart in a concise and agreeable form a clear general outline of the history of our great Indian Empire.'—*Economist.*

'A skilful and most attractive picture. . . . The author has made good use of public and private documents, and has enjoyed the privilege of being aided by the deceased statesman's family. His little work is, consequently, a valuable contribution to modern history.'—*Academy.*

'The book should command a wide circle of readers, not only for its author's sake and that of its subject, but partly at least on account of the very attractive way in which it has been published at the moderate price of half-a-crown. But it is, of course, by its intrinsic merits alone that a work of this nature should be judged. And those merits are everywhere conspicuous. . . . A writer whose thorough mastery of all Indian subjects has been acquired by years of practical experience and patient research.'—*The Athenæum.*

'Never have we been so much impressed by the great literary abilities of Sir William Hunter as we have been by the perusal of "The Marquess of Dalhousie." . . . The knowledge displayed by the writer of the motives of Lord Dalhousie's action, of the inner working of his mind, is so complete, that Lord Dalhousie himself, were he living, could not state them more clearly. . . . Sir William Hunter's style is so clear, his language so vivid, and yet so simple, conveying the impressions he wishes so perspicuously that they cannot but be understood, that the work must have a place in every library, in every home, we might say indeed every cottage.'—*Evening News.*

'Sir William Hunter has written an admirable little volume on "The Marquess of Dalhousie" for his series of the "Rulers of India." It can be read at a sitting, yet its references—expressed or implied—suggest the study and observation of half a life-time.'—*The Daily News.*

Opinions of the Press

ON

SIR WILLIAM HUNTER'S 'LORD MAYO.'

'Sir William W. Hunter has contributed a brief but admirable biography of the Earl of Mayo to the series entitled "Rulers of India," edited by himself (Oxford, at the Clarendon Press).'—*The Times.*

'In telling this story in the monograph before us, Sir William Hunter has combined his well-known literary skill with an earnest sympathy and fulness of knowledge which are worthy of all commendation. . . . The world is indebted to the author for a fit and attractive record of what was eminently a noble life.'—*The Academy.*

'The sketch of The Man is full of interest, drawn as it is with complete sympathy, understanding, and appreciation. But more valuable is the account of his administration. No one can show so well and clearly as Sir William Hunter does what the policy of Lord Mayo contributed to the making of the Indian Empire of to-day.'—*The Scotsman.*

'Sir William Hunter has given us a monograph in which there is a happy combination of the essay and the biography. We are presented with the main features of Lord Mayo's administration unencumbered with tedious details which would interest none but the most official of Anglo-Indians; while in the biography the man is brought before us, not analytically, but in a life-like portrait.'—*Vanity Fair.*

'The story of his life Sir W. W. Hunter tells in well-chosen language—clear, succinct, and manly. Sir W. W. Hunter is in sympathy with his subject, and does full justice to Mayo's strong, genuine nature. Without exaggeration and in a direct, unaffected style, as befits his theme, he brings the man and his work vividly before us.'—*The Glasgow Herald.*

'All the knowledge acquired by personal association, familiarity with administrative details of the Indian Government, and a strong grasp of the vast problems to be dealt with, is utilised in this presentation of Lord Mayo's personality and career. Sir W. Hunter, however, never overloads his pages, and the outlines of the sketch are clear and firm.'—*The Manchester Express.*

'This is another of the "Rulers of India" series, and it will be hard to beat. . . . Sir William Hunter's perception and expression are here at their very best.'—*The Pall Mall Gazette.*

'The latest addition to the "Rulers of India" series yields to none of its predecessors in attractiveness, vigour, and artistic portraiture. . . . The final chapter must either be copied verbally and literally—which the space at our disposal will not permit—or be left to the sorrowful perusal of the reader. The man is not to be envied who can read it with dry eyes.'—*Allen's Indian Mail.*

'The little volume which has just been brought out is a study of Lord Mayo's career by one who knew all about it and was in full sympathy with it. . . . Some of these chapters are full of spirit and fire. The closing passages, the picture of the Viceroy's assassination, cannot fail to make any reader hold his breath. We know what is going to happen, but we are thrilled as if we did not know it, and were still held in suspense. The event itself was so terribly tragic that any ordinary description might seem feeble and laggard. But in this volume we are made to feel as we must have felt if we had been on the spot and seen the murderer "fastened like a tiger" on the back of the Viceroy.'—*Daily News*, Leading Article.

Opinions of the Press

ON

MR. W. S. SETON-KARR'S 'CORNWALLIS.'

'This new volume of the "Rulers of India" series keeps up to the high standard set by the author of "The Marquess of Dalhousie." For dealing with the salient passages in Lord Cornwallis's Indian career no one could have been better qualified than the whilom foreign secretary to Lord Lawrence.'—*The Athenæum.*

'Lord Cornwallis has been very properly included in the list of those "Rulers of India" whose biographies are calculated to illustrate the past growth and present development of the English administration in that country. His name is connected with several great measures, which more, perhaps, than any others have given a special colour to our rule, have influenced the course of subsequent legislation, and have made the Civil Service what it at present is. He completed the administrative fabric of which Warren Hastings, in the midst of unexampled difficulties and vicissitudes, had laid the foundation.'—*The Saturday Review.*

'We hope that the volumes on the "Rulers of India" which are being published by the Clarendon Press are carefully read by a large section of the public. There is a dense wall of ignorance still standing between the average Englishman and the greatest dependency of the Crown; although we can scarcely hope to see it broken down altogether, some of these admirable biographies cannot fail to lower it a little. . . . Mr. Seton-Karr has succeeded in the task, and he has not only presented a large mass of information, but he has brought it together in an attractive form. . . . We strongly recommend the book to all who wish to enlarge the area of their knowledge with reference to India.'—*New York Herald.*

'The "Rulers of India" series. This outcome of the Clarendon Press grows in value as it proceeds. The account of Cornwallis is from the pen of Mr. W. Seton-Karr, who was formerly Foreign Secretary to the Government of India, and whose acquaintance with Eastern affairs has been of obvious service to him in the compilation of this useful manual.'—*The Globe.*

'One might almost say that the history of our great Indian Empire might be read with comparative ease in the excellent "Rulers of India Series," published at the Clarendon Press at Oxford. . . . Of Cornwallis it might be said he transformed the East India Company's servants from merchants to administrators, and determined to place them above jobbery, which he despised.'—*The Independent.*

'We have already expressed our sense of the value and timeliness of the series of Indian historical retrospects now issuing, under the editorship of Sir W. W. Hunter, from the Clarendon Press. It is somewhat less than fair to say of Mr. Seton-Karr's monograph upon Cornwallis that it reaches the high standard of literary workmanship which that series has maintained. . . . His accurate and lucid summary of the necessities which dictated Cornwallis's policy, and the methods by which he initiated and, to a great extent, effected, the transformation of our rule in India from the lines of an Oriental despotism to those with which we are now familiar, is as attractive as it is instructive.'—*The Literary World.*

Opinions of the Press

ON

COLONEL MALLESON'S 'DUPLEIX.'

'In the character of Dupleix there was the element of greatness that contact with India seems to have generated in so many European minds, French as well as English, and a broad capacity for government, which, if suffered to have full play, might have ended in giving the whole of Southern India to France. Even as it was, Colonel Malleson shows how narrowly the prize slipped from French grasp. In 1783 the Treaty of Versailles arrived just in time to save the British power from extinction.'—*Times*.

'One of the best of Sir W. Hunter's interesting and valuable series. Colonel Malleson writes out of the fulness of familiarity, moving with ease over a field which he had long ago surveyed in every nook and corner. To do a small book as well as this on Dupleix has been done, will be recognised by competent judges as no small achievement. When one considers the bulk of the material out of which the little volume has been distilled, one can still better appreciate the labour and dexterity involved in the performance.'—*Academy*.

'A most compact and effective history of the French in India in a little handbook of 180 pages.'—*Nonconformist*.

'Well arranged, lucid and eminently readable, an excellent addition to a most useful series.'—*Record*.

COLONEL MALLESON'S 'AKBAR.'

'Colonel Malleson's interesting monograph on Akbar in the "Rulers of India" (Clarendon Press) should more than satisfy the general reader. Colonel Malleson traces the origin and foundation of the Mughal Empire; and, as an introduction to the history of Muhammadan India, the book leaves nothing to be desired.'—*St. James's Gazette*.

'This volume will, no doubt, be welcomed, even by experts in Indian history, in the light of a new, clear, and terse rendering of an old, but not worn-out theme. It is a worthy and valuable addition to Sir W. Hunter's promising series.'—*Athenæum*.

'Colonel Malleson has broken ground new to the general reader. The story of Akbar is briefly but clearly told, with an account of what he was and what he did, and how he found and how he left India. . . . The native chronicles of the reign are many, and from them it is still possible, as Colonel Malleson has shown, to construct a living portrait of this great and mighty potentate.'—*Scots Observer*.

'The brilliant historian of the Indian Mutiny has been assigned in this volume of the series an important epoch and a strong personality for critical study, and he has admirably fulfilled his task. . . . Alike in dress and style, this volume is a fit companion for its predecessor.'—*Manchester Guardian*.

Opinions of the Press

ON

CAPTAIN TROTTER'S 'WARREN HASTINGS.'

'The publication, recently noticed in this place, of the "Letters, Despatches, and other State Papers preserved in the Foreign Department of the Government of India, 1772–1785," has thrown entirely new light from the most authentic sources on the whole history of Warren Hastings and his government of India. Captain L. J. Trotter's WARREN HASTINGS is accordingly neither inopportune nor devoid of an adequate *raison d'être*. Captain Trotter is well known as a competent and attractive writer on Indian history, and this is not the first time that Warren Hastings has supplied him with a theme.'—*The Times.*

'He has put his best work into this memoir. . . . His work is of distinct literary merit, and is worthy of a theme than which British history presents none nobler. It is a distinct gain to the British race to be enabled, as it now may, to count the great Governor-General among those heroes for whom it need not blush.'—*Scotsman.*

'Captain Trotter has done his work well, and his volume deserves to stand with that on Dalhousie by Sir William Hunter. Higher praise it would be hard to give it.'—*New York Herald.*

'Captain Trotter has done full justice to the fascinating story of the splendid achievements of a great Englishman.'—*Manchester Guardian.*

'A brief but admirable biography of the first Governor-General of India.'—*Newcastle Chronicle.*

'A book which all must peruse who desire to be "up to date" on the subject.'—*The Globe.*

MR. KEENE'S 'MADHAVA RAO SINDHIA.'

'Mr. Keene has the enormous advantage, not enjoyed by every producer of a book, of knowing intimately the topic he has taken up. He has compressed into these 203 pages an immense amount of information, drawn from the best sources, and presented with much neatness and effect.'—*The Globe.*

'Mr. Keene tells the story with knowledge and impartiality, and also with sufficient graphic power to make it thoroughly readable. The recognition of Sindhia in the "Rulers" series is just and graceful, and it cannot fail to give satisfaction to the educated classes of our Indian fellow-subjects.'—*North British Daily Mail.*

'The volume bears incontestable proofs of the expenditure of considerable research by the author, and sustains the reputation he had already acquired by his "Sketch of the History of Hindustan."'—*Freeman's Journal.*

'Among the eighteen rulers of India included in the scheme of Sir William Hunter only five are natives of India, and of these the great Madhoji Sindhia is, with the exception of Akbar, the most illustrious. Mr. H. G. Keene, a well-known and skilful writer on Indian questions, is fortunate in his subject, for the career of the greatest bearer of the historic name of Sindhia covered the exciting period from the capture of Delhi, the Imperial capital, by the Persian Nadir Shah, to the occupation of the same city by Lord Lake. . . . Mr. Keene gives a lucid description of his subsequent policy, especially towards the English when he was brought face to face with Warren Hastings.'—*The Daily Graphic.*

Opinions of the Press

ON

MAJOR-GENERAL SIR OWEN BURNE'S 'CLYDE AND STRATHNAIRN.'

'In "Clyde and Strathnairn," a contribution to Sir William Hunter's excellent "Rulers of India" series (Oxford, at the Clarendon Press), Sir Owen Burne gives a lucid sketch of the military history of the Indian Mutiny and its suppression by the two great soldiers who give their names to his book. The space is limited for so large a theme, but Sir Owen Burne skilfully adjusts his treatment to his limits, and rarely violates the conditions of proportion imposed upon him.' . . . 'Sir Owen Burne does not confine himself exclusively to the military narrative. He gives a brief sketch of the rise and progress of the Mutiny, and devotes a chapter to the Reconstruction which followed its suppression.' . . . '—well written, well proportioned, and eminently worthy of the series to which it belongs.'—*The Times.*

'Sir Owen Burne who, by association, experience, and relations with one of these generals, is well qualified for the task, writes with knowledge, perspicuity, and fairness.'—*Saturday Review.*

'As a brief record of a momentous epoch in India this little book is a remarkable piece of clear, concise, and interesting writing.'—*The Colonies and India.*

'Sir Owen Burne has written this book carefully, brightly, and with excellent judgment, and we in India cannot read such a book without feeling that he has powerfully aided the accomplished editor of the series in a truly patriotic enterprise.'—*Bombay Gazette.*

'The volume on "Clyde and Strathnairn" has just appeared and proves to be a really valuable addition to the series. Considering its size and the extent of ground it covers it is one of the best books about the Indian Mutiny of which we know.'—*Englishman.*

'Sir Owen Burne, who has written the latest volume for Sir William Hunter's "Rulers of India" series, is better qualified than any living person to narrate, from a military standpoint, the story of the suppression of the Indian Mutiny.'—*Daily Telegraph.*

'Sir Owen Burne's book on "Clyde and Strathnairn" is worthy to rank with the best in the admirable series to which it belongs.'—*Manchester Examiner.*

'The book is admirably written; and there is probably no better sketch, equally brief, of the stirring events with which it deals.' *Scotsman.*

'Sir Owen Burne, from the part he played in the Indian Mutiny, and from his long connexion with the Government of India, and from the fact that he was military secretary of Lord Strathnairn both in India and in Ireland, is well qualified for the task which he has undertaken.'—*The Athenæum.*

Opinions of the Press

ON

VISCOUNT HARDINGE'S 'LORD HARDINGE.'

'An exception to the rule that biographies ought not to be entrusted to near relatives. Lord Hardinge, a scholar and an artist, has given us an accurate record of his father's long and distinguished services. There is no filial exaggeration. The author has dealt with some controversial matters with skill, and has managed to combine truth with tact and regard for the feelings of others.'—*The Saturday Review.*

'This interesting life reveals the first Lord Hardinge as a brave, just, able man, the very soul of honour, admired and trusted equally by friends and political opponents. The biographer . . . has produced a most engaging volume, which is enriched by many private and official documents that have not before seen the light.'—*The Anti-Jacobin.*

'Lord Hardinge has accomplished a grateful, no doubt, but, from the abundance of material and delicacy of certain matters, a very difficult task in a workmanlike manner, marked by restraint and lucidity.'—*The Pall Mall Gazette.*

'His son and biographer has done his work with a true appreciation of proportion, and has added substantially to our knowledge of the Sutlej Campaign.'—*Vanity Fair.*

'The present Lord Hardinge is in some respects exceptionally well qualified to tell the tale of the eventful four years of his father's Governor-Generalship.'—*The Times.*

'It contains a full account of everything of importance in Lord Hardinge's military and political career; it is arranged . . . so as to bring into special prominence his government of India; and it gives a lifelike and striking picture of the man.'—*Academy.*

'The style is clear, the treatment dispassionate, and the total result a manual which does credit to the interesting series in which it figures.' —*The Globe.*

'The concise and vivid account which the son has given of his father's career will interest many readers.'—*The Morning Post.*

'Eminently readable for everybody. The history is given succinctly, and the unpublished letters quoted are of real value.'—*The Colonies and India.*

'Compiled from public documents, family papers, and letters, this brief biography gives the reader a clear idea of what Hardinge was, both as a soldier and as an administrator.'—*The Manchester Examiner.*

'An admirable sketch.'—*The New York Herald.*

'The Memoir is well and concisely written, and is accompanied by an excellent likeness after the portrait by Sir Francis Grant.'—*The Queen.*

Opinions of the Press
ON
SIR HENRY CUNNINGHAM'S 'EARL CANNING.'

'Sir Henry Cunningham's rare literary skill and his knowledge of Indian life and affairs are not now displayed for the first time, and he has enjoyed exceptional advantages in dealing with his present subject. Lord Granville, Canning's contemporary at school and colleague in public life and one of his oldest friends, furnished his biographer with notes of his recollections of the early life of his friend. Sir Henry Cunningham has also been allowed access to the Diary of Canning's private secretary, to the Journal of his military secretary, and to an interesting correspondence between the Governor-General and his great lieutenant, Lord Lawrence.'—*The Times.*

'Sir H. S. Cunningham has succeeded in writing the history of a critical period in so fair and dispassionate a manner as to make it almost a matter of astonishment that the motives which he has so clearly grasped should ever have been misinterpreted, and the results which he indicates so grossly misjudged. Nor is the excellence of his work less conspicuous from the literary than from the political and historical point of view.'—*Glasgow Herald.*

'Sir H. S. Cunningham has treated his subject adequately. In vivid language he paints his word-pictures, and with calm judicial analysis he also proves himself an able critic of the actualities, causes, and results of the outbreak, also a temperate, just appreciator of the character and policy of Earl Canning.'—*The Court Journal.*

REV. W. H. HUTTON'S 'MARQUESS WELLESLEY.'

'Mr. Hutton has brought to his task an open mind, a trained historical judgement, and a diligent study of a great body of original material. Hence he is enabled to present a true, authentic, and original portrait of one of the greatest of Anglo-Indian statesmen, doing full justice to his military policy and achievements, and also to his statesmanlike efforts for the organization and consolidation of that Empire which he did so much to sustain.'—*Times.*

'To the admirable candour and discrimination which characterize Mr. Hutton's monograph as an historical study must be added the literary qualities which distinguish it and make it one of the most readable volumes of the series. The style is vigorous and picturesque, and the arrangement of details artistic in its just regard for proportion and perspective. In short, there is no point of view from which the work deserves anything but praise.'—*Glasgow Herald.*

'The Rev. W. H. Hutton has done his work well, and achieves with force and lucidity the task he sets himself: to show how, under Wellesley, the Indian company developed and ultimately became the supreme power in India. To our thinking his estimate of this great statesman is most just.'—*Black and White.*

'Mr. Hutton has told the story of Lord Wellesley's life in an admirable manner, and has provided a most readable book.'—*Manchester Examiner.*

'Mr. Hutton's range of information is wide, his division of subjects appropriate, and his diction scholarly and precise.'—*Saturday Review.*

Opinions of the Press

ON

MR. DEMETRIUS BOULGER'S 'LORD WILLIAM BENTINCK.'

'The "Rulers of India" series has received a valuable addition in the biography of the late Lord William Bentinck. The subject of this interesting memoir was a soldier as well as a statesman. He was mainly instrumental in bringing about the adoption of the overland route and in convincing the people of India that a main factor in English policy was a disinterested desire for their welfare. Lord William's despatches and minutes, several of which are textually reproduced in Mr. Boulger's praiseworthy little book, display considerable literary skill and are one and all State papers of signal worth.'—*Daily Telegraph.*

'Mr. Boulger is no novice in dealing with Oriental history and Oriental affairs, and in the career of Lord William Bentinck he has found a theme very much to his taste, which he treats with adequate knowledge and literary skill.'—*The Times.*

'His frontier policy was conciliatory, but full of foresight. His minute on the subject of Afghanistan and the advance of Russia in Asia may be read with advantage to-day, nearly sixty years after it was written. Similarly, his observations on the armies of India have lost by no means all of their force, and Mr. Boulger has done a public service in printing the document.'—*Daily News.*

'How all this was effected has been clearly and forcibly set forth by Mr. Boulger. Though concisely written, his memoir omits nothing really essential to a thorough understanding and just appreciation of Bentinck's work, and of the results which flowed from it, even after he had ceased to be at the head of Indian affairs. Mr. Boulger's estimate of the statesman is eminently fair and dispassionate, based on a thorough knowledge of his administration in all its details. Altogether the little work is a valuable addition to a most useful series.'—*Glasgow Herald.*

'Mr. Boulger writes clearly and well, and his volume finds an accepted place in the very useful and informing series which Sir William Wilson Hunter is editing so ably.'—*Independent.*

'Lord William Bentinck occupies a distinct place among Indian Governors-General. His rule may be regarded as the commencement of an epoch. Mr. Boulger has not to tell a stirring story of war and conquest, but the record of Lord William Bentinck's domestic reforms, by which he began the regeneration of India, is as deeply interesting and certainly as well worth studying as any chapter of preceding Indian history. Mr. Boulger has produced an excellent brief history of the period, and a capital life of the Governor-General. The volume is one of the series of "Rulers of India," and none of them is better worthy of perusal.'—*The Scotsman.*

'Mr. Boulger, it should be added, has done his work with care and judgement.'—*The Globe.*

Opinions of the Press

ON

SIR LEPEL GRIFFIN'S 'RANJIT SINGH.'

'Sir Lepel Griffin treats his topic with thorough mastery, and his account of the famous Mahárájá and his times is, consequently, one of the most valuable as well as interesting volumes of the series of which it forms a part.'—*The Globe.*

'We can thoroughly praise Sir Lepel Griffin's work as an accurate and appreciative account of the beginnings and growth of the Sikh religion and of the temporal power founded upon it by a strong and remorseless chieftain.'—*The Times.*

'One of the best books recently published on any Indian question.'—*The Manchester Guardian.*

'The reading public has here the essence of all that is worth knowing about the period.'—*The Glasgow Evening News.*

'From first to last it is a model of what such a work should be, and a classic. The book is one of the most interesting historical sketches ever given to the public, and illustrated throughout by a unique acquaintance with the subject, and exquisite point.'—*The St. Stephen's Review.*

'Sir Lepel has done justice to one of the most interesting and picturesque episodes of Indian history. In every respect, but perhaps most of all from the point of view of the general reader who does not wholly subordinate enjoyment to instruction, the volume is a most acceptable addition to the series.'—*The Glasgow Herald.*

'The monograph could not have been entrusted to more capable hands than those of Sir Lepel Griffin, who spent his official life in the Punjaub, and is an expert in all the knowledge appertaining to a thorough acquaintance, practical and bookish, with that province. This is an excellent sketch of Ranjit Singh, his people, and his short-lived kingdom.'—*The Scotsman.*

'At once the shortest and best history of the rise and fall of the Sikh monarchy.'—*The North British Daily Mail.*

'An excellent piece of work—candid, discriminating, and well-balanced.'—*The Yorkshire Post.*

'Not only a biography of the Napoleon of the East, but a luminous picture of his country; the chapter on Sikh Theocracy being a notable example of compact thought. For grasp of subject, careful treatment, and charm of narration, this volume is second to none in the series. It may fairly be said to "speak volumes," and possesses an exceptional value as being by our chief authority on Punjab matters.'—*The Liverpool Mercury.*

'The career of no Indian ruler since the Moghul Aurungzebe and the Mahratta Sivaji presents a finer subject for the historian; and it would be difficult to find a writer better qualified than Sir Lepel Griffin to deal with such a subject.'—*The St. James's Gazette.*

'A truly masterly account of Ranjit Singh and the short-lived Sikh monarchy of Lahore.'—*The World.*

'The sketch is in every respect a masterly one, and proves its author to be capable of producing something on a larger scale that would be unsurpassed among histories of our great dependency.'—*The Literary World.*

Opinions of the Press

ON

MR. J. S. COTTON'S 'MOUNTSTUART ELPHINSTONE.'

'Sir William Hunter, the editor of the series to which this book belongs, was happily inspired when he entrusted the Life of Elphinstone, one of the most scholarly of Indian rulers, to Mr. Cotton, who, himself a scholar of merit and repute, is brought by the nature of his daily avocations into close and constant relations with scholars. . . . We live in an age in which none but specialists can afford to give more time to the memoirs of even the most distinguished Anglo-Indians than will be occupied by reading Mr. Cotton's two hundred pages. He has performed his task with great skill and good sense. This is just the kind of Life of himself which the wise, kindly, high-souled man, who is the subject of it, would read with pleasure in the Elysian Fields.'—Sir M. E. Grant Duff, in *The Academy*.

'To so inspiring a theme few writers are better qualified to do ample justice than the author of "The Decennial Statement of the Moral and Material Progress and Condition of India." Sir T. Colebrooke's larger biography of Elphinstone appeals mainly to Indian specialists, but Mr. Cotton's slighter sketch is admirably adapted to satisfy the growing demand for a knowledge of Indian history and of the personalities of Anglo-Indian statesmen which Sir William Hunter has done so much to create.'—*The Times*.

'This is the story of a brilliant life, brilliantly told. Mr. Cotton has a crisp style, a wide knowledge of Indian history, and a strong sympathy for his hero.'—*The Pall Mall Gazette*.

'Mr. Cotton's "Life of Mountstuart Elphinstone" is one of the most readable of the valuable volumes that have appeared in the series of "Rulers of India." Mr. Cotton has avoided tediousness by the condensation of matter, and has secured the interest and close attention of his reader by a bright and nimble style which carries him along with quite exhilarating rapidity, yet without skipping the really salient features of the period.'—*The Scotsman*.

'Mr. Cotton has evidently performed a congenial task in writing this excellent little biography, for he has produced a volume so pleasant to read that it can scarcely be the result of labour against the grain. He has given us an account of the public career of a man who, though he declined the post of Governor-General, well deserves to rank among the ablest "Rulers of India," and of those literary pursuits which occupied Elphinstone's spare time during his period of office, and bore good and abiding fruit both in his despatches and his historical work.'—*The Journal of Education*.

'The author has evidently taken great pains to make the book what a monograph of the kind ought to be; and those who are familiar with Anglo-Indian history during the early part of the current century will appreciate the praise we offer when we say that he has succeeded in making it worthy of its subject.'—*The World*.

'A masterpiece of skilful and sympathetic workmanship. . . . Such a life could scarcely be told without exciting interest: told as it is by Mr. Cotton, it combines all the qualities of that oft-abused word—fascination.'—*The Queen*.

Opinions of the Press

ON

MR. MORSE STEPHENS' 'ALBUQUERQUE.'

'Mr. Stephens' able and instructive monograph . . . We may commend Mr. Morse Stephens' volume, both as an adequate summary of an important period in the history of the relations between Asia and Europe, and as a suggestive treatment of the problem of why Portugal failed and England succeeded in founding an Indian Empire.'—*The Times.*

'Mr. H. Morse Stephens has made a very readable book out of the foundation of the Portuguese power in India. According to the practice of the series to which it belongs it is called a life of Affonso de Albuquerque, but the Governor is only the central and most important figure in a brief history of the Portuguese in the East down to the time when the Dutch and English intruded on their preserves . . . A pleasantly-written and trustworthy book on an interesting man and time.' —*The Saturday Review.*

'Mr. Morse Stephens' *Albuquerque* is a solid piece of work, well put together, and full of interest.'—*The Athenæum.*

'Mr. Morse Stephens' studies in Indian and Portuguese history have thoroughly well qualified him for approaching the subject . . . He has presented the facts of Albuquerque's career, and sketched the events marking the rule of his predecessor Almeida, and of his immediate successors in the Governorship and Viceroyalty of India in a compact, lucid, and deeply interesting form.'—*The Scotsman.*

SIR CHARLES AITCHISON'S 'LORD LAWRENCE.'

'No man knows the policy, principles, and character of John Lawrence better than Sir Charles Aitchison. The salient features and vital principles of his work as a ruler, first in the Punjab, and afterwards as Viceroy, are set forth with remarkable clearness.'—*Scotsman.*

'A most admirable sketch of the great work done by Sir John Lawrence, who not only ruled India, but saved it.'—*Manchester Examiner.*

'Sir Charles Aitchison's narrative is uniformly marked by directness, order, clearness, and grasp; it throws additional light into certain nooks of Indian affairs; and it leaves upon the mind a very vivid and complete impression of Lord Lawrence's vigorous, resourceful, discerning, and valiant personality.'—*Newcastle Daily Chronicle.*

'Sir Charles knows the Punjab thoroughly, and has made this little book all the more interesting by his account of the Punjab under John Lawrence and his subordinates.'—*Yorkshire Post.*

Opinions of the Press
ON

LEWIN BENTHAM BOWRING'S 'HAIDAR ALÍ AND TIPÚ SULTÁN.'

'Mr. Bowring's portraits are just, and his narrative of the continuous military operations of the period full and accurate.'—*Times.*

'The story has been often written, but never better or more concisely than here, where the father and son are depicted vividly and truthfully "in their habit as they lived." There is not a volume of the whole series which is better done than this, or one which shows greater insight.'—*Daily Chronicle.*

'Mr. Bowring has been well chosen to write this memorable history, because he has had the best means of collecting it, having himself formerly been Chief Commissioner of Mysore. The account of the Mysore war is well done, and Mr. Bowring draws a stirring picture of our determined adversary.'—*Army and Navy Gazette.*

'An excellent example of compression and precision. Many volumes might be written about the long war in Mysore, and we cannot but admire the skill with which Mr. Bowring has condensed the history of the struggle. His book is as terse and concise as a book can be.'—*North British Daily Mail.*

'Mr. Bowring's book is one of the freshest and best of a series most valuable to all interested in the concerns of the British Empire in the East.'—*English Mail.*

'The story of the final capture of Seringapatam is told with skill and graphic power by Mr. Bowring, who throughout the whole work shows himself a most accurate and interesting historian.'—*Perthshire Advertiser.*

COLONEL MALLESON'S 'LORD CLIVE.'

'This book gives a spirited and accurate sketch of a very extraordinary personality.'—*Speaker.*

'Colonel Malleson writes a most interesting account of Clive's great work in India—so interesting that, having begun to read it, one is unwilling to lay it aside until the last page has been reached. The character of Clive as a leader of men, and especially as a cool, intrepid, and resourceful general, is ably described; and at the same time the author never fails to indicate the far-reaching political schemes which inspired the valour of Clive and laid the foundation of our Indian Empire.'—*North British Daily Mail.*

'This monograph is admirably written by one thoroughly acquainted and in love with his subject.'—*Glasgow Herald.*

'No one is better suited than Colonel Malleson to write on Clive, and he has performed his task with distinct success. The whole narrative is, like everything Colonel Malleson writes, clear and full of vigour.'—*Yorkshire Post.*

'Colonel Malleson is reliable and fair, and the especial merit of his book is that it always presents a clear view of the whole of the vast theatre in which Clive gradually produces such an extraordinary change of scene.'—*Newcastle Daily Chronicle.*

Opinions of the Press

ON

CAPT. TROTTER'S 'EARL OF AUCKLAND.'

'A vivid account of the causes, conduct, and consequences of "the costly, fruitless, and unrighteous" Afghan War of 1838.'—*St. James's Gazette.*

'To write such a monograph was a thankless task, but it has been accomplished with entire success by Captain L. J. Trotter. He has dealt calmly and clearly with Lord Auckland's policy, domestic and military, with its financial results, and with the general tendency of Lord Auckland's rule.'—*Yorkshire Post.*

'To this distressing story (of the First Afghan War) Captain Trotter devotes the major portion of his pages. He tells it well and forcibly; but is drawn, perhaps unavoidably, into the discussion of many topics of controversy which, to some readers, may seem to be hardly as yet finally decided. . . . It is only fair to add that two chapters are devoted to "Lord Auckland's Domestic Policy," and to his relations with "The Native States of India".'—*The Times.*

'Captain Trotter's *Earl of Auckland* is a most interesting book, and its excellence as a condensed, yet luminous, history of the first Afghan War deserves warm recognition.'—*Scotsman.*

'It points a moral which our Indian Rulers cannot afford to forget so long as they still have Russia and Afghanistan to count with.'—*Glasgow Herald.*

Supplementary Volume: price 3s. 6d.

'JAMES THOMASON,' BY SIR RICHARD TEMPLE.

'Sir R. Temple's book possesses a high value as a dutiful and interesting memorial of a man of lofty ideals, whose exploits were none the less memorable because achieved exclusively in the field of peaceful administration.'—*Times.*

'It is the peculiar distinction of this work that it interests a reader less in the official than in the man himself.'—*Scotsman.*

'This is a most interesting book: to those who know India, and knew the man, it is of unparalleled interest, but no one who has the Imperial instinct which has taught the English to rule subject races "for their own welfare" can fail to be struck by the simple greatness of this character.'—*Pall Mall Gazette.*

'Mr. Thomason was a great Indian statesman. He systematized the revenue system of the North-West Provinces, and improved every branch of the administration. He was remarkable, like many great Indians, for the earnestness of his religious faith, and Sir Richard Temple brings this out in an admirable manner.'—*British Weekly.*

'The book is "a portrait drawn by the hand of affection," of one whose life was "a pattern of how a Christian man ought to live." Special prominence is given to the religious aspects of Mr. Thomason's character, and the result is a very readable biographical sketch.'—*Christian.*

Opinions of the Press

ON

MAJOR ROSS OF BLADENSBURG'S 'MARQUESS OF HASTINGS.'

'Major Ross of Bladensburg treats his subject skilfully and attractively, and his biography of Lord Hastings worthily sustains the high reputation of the Series in which it appears.'—*The Times.*

'This monograph is entitled to rank with the best of the Series, the compiler having dealt capably and even brilliantly with his materials.' —*English Mail.*

'Instinct with interest.'—*Glasgow Evening News.*

'As readable as it is instructive.'—*Globe.*

'A truly admirable monograph.'—*Glasgow Herald.*

'Major Ross has done his work admirably, and bids fair to be one of the best writers the Army of our day has given to the country. . . . A most acceptable and entrancing little volume.'—*Daily Chronicle.*

'It is a volume that merits the highest praise. Major Ross of Bladensburg has represented Lord Hastings and his work in India in the right light, faithfully described the country as it was, and in a masterly manner makes one realize how important was the period covered by this volume.'—*Manchester Courier.*

'This excellent monograph ought not to be overlooked by any one who would fully learn the history of British rule in India.'—*Manchester Examiner.*

MR. S. LANE-POOLE'S 'AURANGZÍB.'

'There is no period in Eastern history so full of sensation as the reign of Aurangzíb. . . . Mr. Lane-Poole tells this story admirably; indeed, it were difficult to imagine it better told.'—*National Observer.*

'Mr. Lane-Poole writes learnedly, lucidly, and vigorously. . . . He draws an extremely vivid picture of Aurangzíb, his strange ascetic character, his intrepid courage, his remorseless overthrow of his kinsmen, his brilliant court, and his disastrous policy; and he describes the gradual decline of the Mogul power from Akbar to Aurangzíb with genuine historical insight.'—*Times.*

'A well-knit and capable sketch of one of the most remarkable, perhaps the most interesting, of the Mogul Emperors.'—*Saturday Review.*

'As a study of the man himself, Mr. Lane-Poole's work is marked by a vigour and originality of thought which give it a very exceptional value among works on the subject.'—*Glasgow Herald.*

'The most popular and most picturesque account that has yet appeared . . . a picture of much clearness and force.'—*Globe.*

'A notable sketch, at once scholarly and interesting.'—*English Mail.*

'No one is better qualified than Mr. Stanley Lane-Poole to take up the history and to depict the character of the last of the great Mogul monarchs. . . . Aurangzíb's career is ever a fascinating study.'—*Home News.*

'The author gives a description of the famous city of Sháh Jahán, its palaces, and the ceremonies and pageants of which they were the scene. . . . Mr. Lane-Poole's well-written monograph presents all the most distinctive features of Aurangzíb's character and career.'—*Morning Post.*

Uniform with the 'Rulers of India' Series, 3s. 6d.

A BRIEF HISTORY OF THE INDIAN PEOPLES.

STANDARD EDITION (TWENTIETH), REVISED TO 1892.
SEVENTY-EIGHTH THOUSAND.

This Edition incorporates the suggestions received by the author from Directors of Public Instruction and other educational authorities in India; its statistics are brought down to the Census of 1891; and its narrative, to 1892. The work has received the emphatic approval of the organ of the English School Boards, and has been translated into five languages. It is largely employed for educational purposes in Europe and America and as a text-book prescribed by the University of Calcutta for its Entrance Examination from 1886 to 1891.

'"A Brief History of the Indian Peoples," by W. W. Hunter, presents a sort of bird's-eye view both of India and of its people from the earliest dawn of historical records . . . . A work of authority and of original value.'—*The Daily News* (London).

'Dr. Hunter may be said to have presented a compact epitome of the results of his researches into the early history of India; a subject upon which his knowledge is at once exceptionally wide and exceedingly thorough.'—*The Scotsman.*

'Within the compass of some 250 pages we know of no history of the people of India so concise, so interesting, and so useful for educational purposes as this.'—*The School Board Chronicle* (London).

'For its size and subject there is not a better written or more trustworthy history in existence.'—*The Journal of Education.*

'So thoroughly revised as to entitle it to separate notice.'—*The Times.*

'Dr. Hunter's history, if brief, is comprehensive. It is a storehouse of facts marshalled in a masterly style; and presented, as history should be, without the slightest suspicion of prejudice or suggestion of partisanship. Dr. Hunter observes a style of severe simplicity, which is the secret of an impressive presentation of details.'—*The Daily Review* (Edinburgh).

'By far the best manual of Indian History that has hitherto been published, and quite equal to any of the Historical Series for Schools edited by Dr. Freeman. We trust that it will soon be read in all the schools in this Presidency.'—*The Times of India.*

Extract from a criticism by Edward Giles, Esq., Inspector of Schools, Northern Division, Bombay Presidency:—'What we require is a book which shall be accurate as to facts, but not overloaded with them; written in a style which shall interest, attract, and guide uncultivated readers; and short, because it must be sold at a reasonable price. These conditions have never, in my opinion, been realized previous to the introduction of this book.'

'The publication of the Hon. W. W. Hunter's "School History of India" is an event in literary history.'—*Reis & Rayyet* (Calcutta).

'He has succeeded in writing a history of India, not only in such a way that it will be read, but also in a way which we hope will lead young Englishmen and young natives of India to think more kindly of each other. The Calcutta University has done wisely in prescribing this brief history as a text-book for the Entrance Examination.'—*The Hindoo Patriot* (Calcutta).